A Practical Program
for America

A
Practical Program
for America

EDITED BY HENRY HAZLITT

Essay Index Reprint Series

BOOKS FOR LIBRARIES PRESS, INC.
FREEPORT, NEW YORK

First published 1932
Reprinted 1967

HC106.3
.H395
1967

Editor's Note

EACH of the authors of the following essays, which
appeared originally in *The Nation*, has set forth
what he believes would be the most desirable program
for America to follow in the next four years in some
particular phase of our economic life. Though the difficulties of a literal compliance were recognized, each
contributor was asked wherever possible to make his
suggestions almost as specific as if he were drawing up
a bill to be presented to Congress. The decision to keep
a relatively short period like the next four years prin-
cipally in mind, it was felt, would save the essays from
utopianism or vagueness, and the fact that each writer
confined himself to some one phase of our economic
life—in most cases that phase in which he had specialized for many years—would be a further assurance
of definiteness and practicality.

"The efforts of the human intellect," Morris R.
Cohen has admirably remarked, "may be viewed as a
tension between two poles—one to do justice to the full-
ness of the concrete case before us, the other to grasp
an underlying abstract universal principle that controls
much more than the one case before us." Recent popular
economic discussion, unfortunately, has been swinging
too far to the second pole—and most of it has remained
there. We are told by one group that we must at all
costs avoid "socialistic experiments," or any undermin-
ing of our heritage of "rugged individualism"; we are

v

told by another that "capitalism" is doomed, and that all change is insignificant and niggling unless it means the complete destruction of a "class" society in favor of a "classless" society. In between are those who advocate "planning," and tell us that "competition" must pass in favor of "control." These general terms, on which so much oratory can be built, begin to seem of doubtful utility when we are confronted with concrete situations. Economic problems are complicated and difficult; they cannot be solved by slogans. We may talk glibly of "planning" when we talk in general terms, but not until we ask ourselves precisely what we are to do with our banks, our farms, or our railroads, do we grapple with our real problems or realize keenly just what those problems are.

This realistic and concrete approach we believe to be one of the merits of a symposium of the present type compared with a volume in which any one writer attempts to apply some single formula to the whole economic field. It would be foolish to pretend that this little book itself deals completely with that field. Unavoidably, some of the subjects overlap to a slight extent, and there are obvious gaps. Banking, agriculture, utilities, railroads, housing, are considered separately. But what, it may be asked, of the desperately needed control of the petroleum industry? What of coal? What of the regulation of the stock exchanges and security flotation? And if unemployment insurance is included, what of old-age pensions, the minimum wage, the whole range of labor problems? All that can be said is that separate consideration of every topic of this sort would have meant a very bulky volume, if not many volumes.

What the symposium does, in effect, is to consider ten sample problems that happen also to be key problems.

No attempt was made to impose any particular point of view on the contributors, nor was it expected that as a group they would reveal any completely unified economic philosophy. Yet the beliefs and attitudes they hold in common are much more extensive and impressive than their differences. All of them see the necessity for broader and more intelligent social control. None of them puts his faith in violence. Each of them, whether his private ideal happens to be a healthier and more stable capitalism or the ultimate annihilation of the profit system, recognizes that our crucial economic problems cannot be solved without specialized knowledge and much patient piecemeal study.

H. H.

Contents

x

A Practical Program
for America

HENRY HAZLITT

is an associate editor of The Nation. *He was formerly economist of the Mechanics and Metals National Bank (New York), American correspondent of the* Revue economique internationale *(Belgium), and financial editor of the New York* Evening Mail.

World Action
for World Recovery

NOTHING is more calculated to lead the student of economics to throw up his hands in complete despair, than a mere recital of the present actual economic policies of governments. What possible point can there be, he is likely to ask, in discussing refinements and advances in economic theory, when popular thought and the actual policies of governments, certainly in everything connected with international relations, have not yet caught up with Adam Smith? For the present-day tariff policy of Europe and America is hardly distinguishable from the tariff policies rampant in the seventeenth and eighteenth centuries. The real reasons for those tariffs are the same, and the pretended reasons are also the same.

In the century and a half since "The Wealth of Nations" appeared, the case for free trade has been stated thousands of times, but probably never with more direct simplicity and force than it was stated in that volume. In general Smith rested his case on one fundamental proposition: "In every country it always is and must be the interest of the great body of the people to buy whatever they want of those who sell it cheapest." "The proposition is so very manifest," Smith continued, "that

3

it seems ridiculous to take any pains to prove it; nor could it ever have been called in question, had not the interested sophistry of merchants and manufacturers confounded the common-sense of mankind." From another point of view, free trade was considered as one aspect of the specialization of labor:

"It is the maxim of every prudent master of a family, never to attempt to make at home what it will cost him more to make than to buy. The tailor does not attempt to make his own shoes, but buys them of the shoemaker. The shoemaker does not attempt to make his own clothes, but employs a tailor. The farmer attempts to make neither the one nor the other, but employs those different artificers. All of them find it for their interest to employ their whole industry in a way in which they have some advantage over their neighbors, and to purchase with a part of its produce, or what is the same thing, with the price of a part of it, whatever else they have occasion for. What is prudence in the conduct of every private family can scarce be folly in that of a great kingdom."

One of the most stubborn notions which Adam Smith had to combat was that identifying "money" with wealth.

"That wealth consists in money, or in gold and silver, is a popular notion which naturally arises from the double function of money, as the instrument of commerce, and as the measure of value. . . . To grow rich is to get money; and wealth and money, in short, are, in common language, considered as in every respect

4

synonymous. A rich country, in the same manner as a rich man, is supposed to be a country abounding in money; and to heap up gold and silver in any country is supposed to be the readiest way to enrich it."

This whole notion, as Smith had little trouble in showing, was a childish one; it rested upon a mere verbal ambiguity; and yet so firmly intrenched had it become that even those "who are convinced of its absurdity, are very apt to forget their own principles, and in the course of their reasonings to take it for granted as a certain and undeniable truth." The notion, unfortunately, seems as solidly imbedded in popular thought in 1932 as it was in 1776. On no other ground can we explain the pathological fear in nearly every nation today, not merely of an "unfavorable" balance of trade, but of imports of any kind that could possibly be made, at no matter what added cost, at home. The statesmen of the world in whose hands our destinies have been placed stand in their economic thought exactly where the mercantilists stood in the seventeenth century. A hundred and fifty-six years after Adam Smith produced his masterly argument for free trade, his countrymen are being humbugged by the infantile slogan "Buy British"; while the United States, which as the greatest creditor nation in the world has more reason than ever for reducing its tariffs if it ever hopes to have its loans repaid, maintains the most preposterous tariff system in existence.

It is frequently pretended that there are now reasons for high tariffs which the knowledge and conditions of Adam Smith's time did not enable him to see. It would

5

be interesting to know what these reasons are. Smith was certainly familiar with the "infant industries" argument: he admits that a specific tariff may hasten the establishment of this or that industry, though he gives strong reasons for doubting whether in the long run a nation as a whole is any better off on that account. Certainly, in any case, the "infant industries" argument is an absurd one in the United States of today. Smith concedes, also, that it may be advisable to protect by tariff certain industries essential to the national defense, though he also makes it clear that from any other standpoint such an indirect subsidy is just as much an unproductive economic burden as the expenditures for the army and navy. Nor was Smith even unfamiliar with the argument prevalent in every European country today, that tariffs were necessary as "retaliatory" measures, or for purposes of "bargaining." On the contrary, he found it necessary to relate the history of the purely retaliatory tariffs during the century before he wrote, as well as the wars they led to. And he conceded that retaliations of this kind might even be good policy if there was a genuine probability that they would procure the repeal of the high duties or prohibitions complained of. But he added:

"When there is no probability that any such repeal can be procured, it seems a bad method of compensating the injury done to certain classes of our people, to do another injury ourselves, not only to those classes, but to almost all the other classes of them. . . . Those workmen who suffered by our neighbors' prohibition will not be benefited by ours. On the contrary, they and

6

almost all the other classes of our citizens will thereby be obliged to pay dearer than before for certain goods."

And, as he remarked, tariffs imposed through sheer animosity are almost certain to be even more irrational than those imposed through the greed of manufacturers.

If the shade of Adam Smith were to revisit this planet today, I doubt whether it would be greatly shocked or astonished by the tariff policies it saw in practice. Adam Smith in the flesh had trained himself to hope for very little. "To expect, indeed," he wrote in his great book, "that the freedom of trade should ever be entirely restored in Great Britain, is as absurd as to expect that an Oceana or Utopia should ever be established in it. Not only the prejudices of the public, but what is much more unconquerable, the private interests of many individuals, irresistibly oppose it."

I quote "The Wealth of Nations" at this length, mainly to show how pathetically little progress the statesmen and the masses of the world have made in their economic thinking, which, as I have said, is in all international matters still at the level of the seventeenth century; but it is by no means to be inferred that the problem of tariffs is of no more importance in 1932 than it was in 1776. On the contrary, both technological progress and the circumstances of the last few years make tariff reduction one of the two or three most desperately urgent economic needs of the moment.

The effect of technical progress ought to be too obvious to need dwelling upon. The enormous increase in transportation facilities, in railroads, motor trucks, fast ocean freight, and so forth; the ease and immediacy of

7

communication by letter, telephone, and cable; the growth of international markets, like that at Liverpool, where a minute change of price may effect within an hour or two a corresponding change of price for the same commodity in every other great market of the world; the growth of international banking transactions; the daily shifting of balances; the hourly adjustment of foreign-exchange rates—all these have combined to make the world increasingly a single economic organism, of which the individual nations are at bottom merely interdependent cells. This statement seems like a mere truism, but one finds no evidence in any important country of the world of any general policy based on the assumption that it is true. The actual policies of nearly every leading nation have been based on precisely the opposite assumption— that each nation is a self-contained economic unit. Indeed, in the face of what is with appalling obviousness the greatest *world* crisis in a century—when a financial panic originating in Austria swept through Hungary and Germany, then to Britain and the Scandinavian countries, and finally to the United States—when the indices of production, unemployment, and prices have in every country been moving in the same direction, and even to almost exactly the same degree (for example, in March, 1932, average wholesale prices in the United States stood at 66 per cent of their 1926 level, in Canada at 69 per cent, in Great Britain at 71 per cent, in France at 64 per cent, in Germany at 74 per cent)—in the face of all this, the President of the United States is capable of continuing to talk about our "self-containment," and of letting it be known that he "will devote

8

his entire time to the domestic problems of the United States," and let Europe stew in its own juice.

The plain truth is that the pivotal business of the world today is everywhere conducted, not in separate national markets, but in what is, in effect, one great international market. Wheat, cotton, copper, petroleum, wool, silk, rubber, coffee, sugar, silver, gold—all are "international" commodities; their price is determined not by local or national but by world shortages or surpluses, and a violent change in the price of any of them sends its repercussions through the whole business structure. The simple statement that our foreign trade is 10 to 15 per cent of our total trade does not indicate its real importance to us. It does not mean that we should be 85 to 90 per cent as well off if our foreign trade stopped altogether. We have to remember, first, that even a 5 per cent drop in the total demand for a commodity may mean a decline of 25 per cent or more in the price of that commodity, and that such a price decline may turn a general profit for the producers into a general loss. And we have to remember, second, that this 10 to 15 per cent is an *average* figure, and does not tell the story of any one commodity. More than one-half of all our cotton, for example, is ordinarily sent abroad; the sudden wiping out of our foreign trade would mean the ruin of the South.

Social causation is nearly always complex, and it is seldom that any given economic situation can be ascribed to any one single factor, but it is as clear as economic evidence can be that, second only to the war itself, the present depression is largely the result of the world's tariff walls, and particularly the tariff of the United

9

States. One striking evidence of this was the violent collapse of the speculative markets as the preposterous Hawley-Smoot tariff advanced toward passage, a collapse which the proponents of the bill denounced at the time as a "Wall Street plot." Since then all the world's business has evidently joined the conspiracy to discredit that tariff. In the days before the war it was still possible for us to prosper in spite of high tariffs, but this situation altered abruptly when we were changed by the war from a debtor nation to the world's foremost creditor nation, and when it became absolutely necessary for us to increase our imports if the debts owed to us were to be paid. Though even the former Fordney-McCumber tariff was far too high, its ill effects were disguised by the fact that we began selling goods to Europe on a tremendous scale *on credit*. We not only refused on net balance to accept the interest on our former loans, but we extended in a few years billions of dollars of new loans. And then, quite suddenly, we stopped. The collapse of our own security markets made us panic-stricken. We no longer had enough faith in the rest of the world to extend it credit, and we did not feel we could spare the credit anyway. We wanted our money. We wanted a real liquidation of the debts. We wanted the outside world to pay the interest on its old debts out of its own resources, and not out of fresh loans. And instead of lowering the tariff to permit the outside world to do this, we raised it.

The effect of a tariff is always to subsidize inefficiency. A tariff is a device for insuring that a commodity which could be bought at a lower cost from abroad shall be produced at a higher cost at home. But when a given tariff level has been established for a long time, an adjustment to it is usually achieved, and a country can prosper at that artificial equilibrium. When tariffs are constantly and rapidly being raised all over the world, however, even this artificial equilibrium is not possible. It has been made doubly impossible at present by another factor, the violent fall of commodity prices. This is relatively unimportant in the case of those commodities which are subject to ad valorem tariffs, but supremely important in the case of those subject to specific tariffs. Thus in 1928, when duty-paid raw sugar was selling in New York at an average price of 4.22 cents a pound, the specific tariff of 1.75 cents a pound on Cuban sugar meant an ad valorem tariff of 70 per cent; at the price levels of Cuban duty-paid sugar in May of this year—2.58 cents a pound—the specific tariff, now raised to 2 cents a pound on Cuban sugar, meant an ad valorem tariff of 345 per cent!

It need hardly be said that an immediate reduction of world tariffs is now imperative. The United States, which took the leadership in raising them, must take the leadership in reducing them. Because the need for tariff reduction is general, there has been a growing belief that the end can be best achieved by an international conference. The present writer cannot subscribe to this belief. There is, to begin with, no possible basis of bargaining or exchange in such matters. If the aim proposed, for example, were that each nation should reduce its tariffs by 25 per cent, any nation could raise its tariff by 100 per cent or any other extravagant figure just before going into the conference. Tariffs, again, are not general, but specific; the tariff on each article is considered ostensibly on its own merits; and any bargaining, article for article, would be endlessly and hopelessly complicated. If an agreement were in spite of all finally arrived at, the various parliaments would have to pass on it in any case. Finally, the basic assumption of such a conference would be the thoroughly false one that tariff walls are beneficial to the countries that put them up and injurious only to foreigners, and that the lowering of tariffs represents "concessions" or "sacrifices" made by each nation merely for the good of the rest. Congress would be asked to reduce the tariff not as an essential need of our own but as a favor to Europe.

A far more direct, honest, and realistic path is for each country to act for itself. America must take the lead. A reduction of our tariff would be an enormous gain to us whether any other nation followed or not. I do not mean that we should return immediately to free trade, assuming that were politically conceivable. Even Adam Smith was careful to point out that "every such [tariff] regulation introduces some degree of real disorder into the constitution of the State, which it will be difficult afterward to cure without occasioning another disorder." Our immediate aim should be rather to approach our former equilibrium than to try to establish a new one. This could be achieved most nearly, perhaps, by a tariff reduction averaging somewhere between 25 and 50 per cent.

It is impossible to consider the tariff without considering international debts. The real problem of those debts is the problem of the international transfer of goods. In arguing against the cancellation or even the reduction of the European debts to our government,

12

Senator Borah—before his later striking and heartening change of view—remarked that the annual payments on our debt called for only 2.45 per cent of the total budget of Belgium, only 3.75 per cent of that of Great Britain, only 1.41 per cent of that of Italy, and only 2.65 per cent of that of France. But he had nothing whatever to say of the far more relevant problem of transfer—of how Europe could secure a sufficient excess of exports to us over imports from us to make these payments possible, of whether we should be willing to lower our tariffs sufficiently to take this excess, of precisely what goods this excess would consist in, or of whether he would prefer to see the excess achieved merely by Europe's reducing by that much its purchases of American commodities.

What makes the settlement of the war debts a question of such immediate moment, however, is the problem of German reparations. Even the French have finally come to see that the reparations burden imposed on Germany by the Young Plan was not only a staggering load on the German taxpayer but far larger than Germany could be expected to meet out of an export surplus. The payments up to the time of the Hoover moratorium were made possible only by fresh outside borrowing—a simple borrowing from Peter to pay Paul —and it is now everywhere recognized that that process has come to an end. The official recognition came at Lausanne when the Allied Governments agreed to reduce the reparations to the comparatively negligible capital amount of $715,000,000, about one-tenth of the total of payments called for under the Young Plan. It is true that this was done only with the "gentleman's agreement" that the settlement would not be ratified by the Allied parliaments until a corresponding reduction was made in their debts to the United States. The publication of this understanding created much righteous indignation in the breasts of many American Senators, but there was no rational reason why it should have done so. Had any realist seriously expected that France and her allies would consent practically to wipe out reparations unless their debts to the United States were similarly canceled or reduced? Did he really believe that we could say in effect to France, England, and Italy, "For the sake of restoring economic stability in the world you must practically wipe out reparations. For the sake of world stability you must make this sacrifice. In return, of course, you cannot hope to have us sacrifice one penny of our claims on you"?

It is worse than stupid, in brief, for us to keep on insisting that reparations are "purely Europe's problem." Wholly apart from any considerations of justice or humanitarianism, we must cancel or drastically cut down the debts for the most cold-blooded of business reasons. Our national income in 1929 was estimated at $84,000,000,000. On the basis of present indices of trade and employment that income appears to have shrunk to a present rate of about $56,000,000,000—a loss of about $28,000,000,000 a year. The debt payments to us amount, in all, to $270,000,000 annually. Is it worth while to sacrifice $28,000,000,000—or even one-tenth that sum—for the sake of $270,000,000? Is it worth while to lose $100, or even $10, for every dollar one collects—assuming one can really collect even that dollar?

14

The reduction of tariffs and the cancellation of the international debts are, then, the two most urgent moves necessary for world recovery. When these have been achieved, other forms of international economic coöperation may be possible—looking, for example, perhaps toward a conference to consider international monetary problems, or toward some measure of international control of raw materials. A beginning might be made by the appointment of a Permanent International Economic Board to make annual and special reports, to sound a warning—before it is too late—when any country or group of countries engages in policies that threaten world stability, and to recommend various forms of coöperation. At first such a board would have to depend for its effectiveness purely on the prestige and moral force of its opinion. Ultimately, of course, we must move toward something better than this. A world that has become a single economic organism cannot continue indefinitely to be controlled by seventy different political sovereignties, each of which, when it is not trying to prosper at its neighbors' expense, tries to pretend that it exists in an economic vacuum.

EDWIN R. A. SELIGMAN

is editor-in-chief of the Encyclopaedia of the Social Sciences. *He was McVicar professor of economics at Columbia University from 1904-1931. He has served on various State and municipal tax commissions, was expert to the League of Nations committee on economics and finance, 1922-1923, served as expert advisor on taxation to Cuba in 1932 and is the author of* "The Shifting and Incidence of Taxation," "Essays in Taxation," *and other volumes on taxation and general economics.*

Toward a New Tax Program

THE TAX problem has not unexpectedly leaped into the center of the political stage. This is more or less true in every country today, but the problem has perhaps nowhere else assumed the significance that it has attained in the United States. Everywhere, indeed, the economic depression has had its fiscal repercussions. The falling off of business activities is quickly reflected in government revenues. There is comparatively little to choose in the matter of elasticity between many kinds of taxes. As business recedes, transactions diminish, consumption is cut down, wages and profits fall, and the reduced incomes are soon capitalized into lower selling values. Customs, excises, stamp duties, corporate and individual income taxes—all suffer the same fate. And while the government revenues recede, the pressure for increased expenditures becomes greater. Emergency outlays for unemployment relief and for direct and indirect subsidies are demanded to such a degree as far to outweigh the pressure for any feasible reduction of expenditures by slashing salaries or lopping off unnecessary outlays. Thus we have the twofold difficulty of a decrease in revenues and an increase in expenditure. The disparity between income and outgo is in periods of depression always greater in the public than in the private economy. The individual in the face of reduced income cuts his expenses to the bone; the government, with even the most laudable intentions of economy, is tempted and often compelled to incur a deficit.

This universal difficulty is aggravated by special causes which are peculiar to the United States. In the first place, the adoption of prohibition has meant a renunciation of what was up to that time a leading source of revenue and of what would otherwise be today a simple and effective method of wiping out almost the entire annual deficit. Secondly, the inclusion of the capital-gains provision in the income-tax law, which unduly swelled the receipts in the fat years, has materially depleted the revenues in the lean years by removing the possibility of charging off capital losses to ordinary income. Thirdly, the reciprocal exemption of State and federal wealth and earnings has become a growing menace to the responsiveness of increased yields to higher rates of taxation. Fourthly, the antiquated system of State and local finance, with its emphasis on the general property tax, is bringing into bold relief the inevitable lag between capital and income values, with a resulting pressure on the small landowner. The consequence of these difficulties, virtually none of which is found in other countries, was the remarkable episode of not many months ago which attended the discussion of the sales tax in Congress, and which fanned the flame of class antagonisms, culminating in what was virtually a political revolution.

Under the circumstances it is necessary to say a word about immediate conditions before discussing the more general problem of the fiscal future which is the proper topic of our reflections. The immediate situation is a result of the deficit, accentuated as it has been by the causes mentioned above. The only way to remove a deficit is to balance the budget, whether national, State, or local. Here two fundamental problems present themselves: How can a budget be balanced and to what period is the balancing to be applied?

To take up the latter point first, it is clear that we must not be too meticulous in defining the period. A budgetary balance is indeed an absolute necessity. For unless the income and outgo correspond, we incur the hazard of either a deficit or a surplus. The danger of the latter is almost equal to that of the former; we have had in the United States on the whole more difficulties with surplus than with deficit financing. While a budget, however, is annual, a budgetary balance is not necessarily restricted to a single year. The requirements of a balanced budget are substantially met if there is an equilibrium after not too protracted a period. In any one year extraordinary occurrences may serve to throw the budget out of gear on the one side or the other. But as long as the inequalities are redressed before untoward consequences emerge, all is well. The dangers, indeed, arise from too long a delay, but there is nothing sacrosanct about a particular twelve months.

If the budgetary period to which the concept of equilibrium applies is fairly prolonged, lean years must be balanced off against the fat ones. This implies a surplus

during the latter. Such a surplus can be either anticipatory or retroactive. To accumulate a surplus because
of a possible future deficit is not easy. With the invin-
cible hopefulness of the taxpayer the pressure will
rather be to dissipate a surplus through tax remissions.
It might, indeed, be possible to provide against unexpected slumps in the revenue by setting up tax reserves
and keeping the rates a little higher than would otherwise be necessary. But the simpler expedient is to make
good the deficit when it actually occurs by borrowing
and then to amortize the loan by securing a subsequent
increase of revenue. The deficit of the past will have
been wiped out by the revenues of the present. The
surplus is retroactive, instead of anticipatory. It is here
that the equilibrium period becomes of importance. In
the case of a huge deficit due to a sudden business depression it would seem unwise to make the balancing
period too short. For this would require both an undue
reduction of outlay and the imposition of heavy taxes
at the precise period when further deflation ought to be
avoided. On the other hand, to keep on borrowing
from year to year without evidence of a resolute will-
ingness to undergo further sacrifice would imperil the
very basis of the public credit. It would still further
undermine the private credit upon which the resumption
of confidence depends.

The principle is illustrated by the crisis through
which we are passing. Were this the first year of the
deficit it would be questionable whether an attempt
should be made to avoid borrowing. But as a matter of
fact we are now in the third year of the depression. In

the first year the deficit was large—nearly three-quarters of a billion dollars. In the second year it was colossal, amounting to about one-half of the ordinary revenues. In this third year it will be still more alarming. Had we not already increased our debt by several billions, a fresh resort to credit might be expedient. But under the actual circumstances it would be hazardous further to prolong the period of balancing. Even at the best it will be several years before the equilibrium for the entire period will have been reached.

The second problem adverted to above is how the budgetary balance, whether short or long time, is to be attained. It is clear that there are four methods of accomplishing the result, three of them looking to the reduction of expenditures, the fourth to the increase of revenues. What appears to be the simplest method is to reduce expenditures directly. This is something which has not yet been seriously attempted in this country. The obstacles are numerous. Obviously, two of the causes of lavish expenditure are war and waste. Far and away the chief elements of modern expenditure are connected with the aftermath of war and the preparation for war. The fiscal preparation for war depends for its reduction upon the adoption of disarmament projects for which world sentiment does not appear to be entirely ripe. The final aftermath of war in the shape of interest and amortization of the debt is well-nigh irreducible; while the difficulties in the way of reducing the grotesque exaggerations of the pension system or veterans' service, whereby large sums are paid to the relatives of men who never saw a day of fighting, are almost insuperable. Yet these war expenditures constitute by all means the most important element in modern government outlay. So far as waste is concerned, the embarrassment arises not so much from the lethargy of mass opinion as from the task of distinguishing between urgent and postponable or between legitimate and extravagant activities. To this must be added not only the reluctance in a period of deflation further to cut down the purchasing power of the community, but also the demands of additional governmental provision for the needy. The net result is the virtually sole reliance upon a drastic cut in public salaries and emoluments—a step which is only beginning to be considered in this country.

The second method of balancing the budget is to reduce expenditures by breaking even in the commercial or primarily business activities of government. The typical examples here are the post office in federal finance, and the subways or water supply in municipal finance. Even in years of abundance it is questionable whether the general taxpayer ought to be saddled with the cost of services which enure to the special benefit of the users. In a period of depression it is particularly indefensible not to make such services carry their own load and become self-supporting. Deficit financing or net outlay in the commercial activities of government is something resolutely to be deprecated.

The third method of reducing expenditures is by suspending the sinking-fund requirements of the debt service. To many this appears to be of doubtful expediency because of the almost sacrosanct character which is presumed to attach to sinking funds. But to financiers who regard the substance rather than the form the issue is not doubtful. Provision for setting up a sinking fund when a loan is created is doubtless expedient as evidence of the good intentions of the government and the desire to strengthen public credit. But unless the sinking fund is automatically alimented by the imposition of a new tax for this purpose, the dependence of the compulsory amortization upon the general revenues of government is illusory. When it becomes necessary to reduce a debt by resort to fresh borrowing, the process is a mere book-keeping device; and if the new loan has to be contracted at a higher rate of interest it becomes absurd. If, on the other hand, the amortization necessitates an increased tax, we are imposing upon the citizens of a particular year not only an unnecessary but an inequitable burden. Far better is it—as was done in our Civil War debt and as is the custom abroad—to treat the sinking-fund provision as something that can be dispensed with in emergencies, and to consider the requirements as substantially fulfilled by amortizing more than the average in good years and less or none in bad years. At the present time in the United States this item alone amounts to several hundred million dollars. Under the pending plans there is no attempt to include it in the deficit to be covered.

When all is said, however, the chief reliance of the budget balancers must be upon an increase of taxation. But it is a great mistake to think of emergency taxation by itself. It was a fateful error of the political leaders in the recent flare-up in Congress to state that the raising of the revenue was more important than the manner in which it was to be raised. The problems are of equal, not of disparate, importance, as recent events have shown. It becomes necessary, therefore, to consider

22

emergency revenue in the light of a normal tax system, especially in view of the fact that several years at least must elapse before an entirely normal tax situation will again have been reached.

Here it is important to keep in mind the various constituents of the tax system. There are in reality three kinds of taxes. While all taxes are ultimately paid by some person, they differ according to the manner of assessment. Taxes may be levied on the person as such irrespective of any particular thing. The chief personal taxes in addition to the poll tax are the general property tax and the general income tax, where the tax is imposed on the person according to his ability to pay, as indicated by his total wealth measured in terms of either property or income. At the other extreme are impersonal taxes, or taxes on things, assessed on the phenomenon irrespective of the person. Such are the ordinary taxes on commodities or transactions, whether on production, on exchange, or on consumption. In between personal and impersonal taxes are those assessed on persons with reference to some particular things, or on things with reference to some particular persons. Such semi-personal taxes are typified by a business tax or a real-estate tax *in rem*. Personal and semi-personal taxes are generally lumped together as direct taxes, in contrast to the impersonal or indirect taxes. A more modern nomenclature is to contrast taxes on wealth and taxes on expenditure, with the stressing of the fiscal aspects in the latter and of the social aspects in the former.

In dealing with the general problem three points emerge. The first is that while democratic progress everywhere emphasizes the growing importance of direct taxes or taxes on wealth, no country has ever been able to rely upon them alone. Indirect taxes formed the exclusive source of our normal federal revenue up to a very recent period, and must continue to supply a substantial share in the future. The chief problem here consists in the choice of such taxes. With the growing emphasis put on their social and economic effects, advanced communities have come to prefer certain classes of indirect taxes. Apart from customs duties, which are everywhere utilized for either fiscal or economic reasons, it has come to be recognized that the least indefensible taxes are imposts on tobacco and drinks, where social and fiscal reasons converge to urge their adoption. Our renunciation, for the time being, of the latter class of taxes has created one of the major difficulties of the present situation. At the other extreme are found the most indefensible revenues, such as the general sales tax which has so violently been rejected by Congress. In between lies a variety of excises which possess in a minor degree the merits of the first class and the demerits of the second.

The next point is the need of envisaging our revenue system as a whole. The old-time simple situation, with federal revenues alimented from indirect taxes and State and local revenues furnished by the general property tax, has disappeared. On the one hand the federal government has had to utilize direct taxes, while the States and localities have not only changed in large measure from personal to semi-personal taxes, but are increasingly compelled to rely upon a different criterion for measuring wealth. The consequence is that federal and

24

State governments are trenching on each other's field. Apart from the constitutional restriction which reserves customs duties to the nation and property taxes to the States, the whole field is open to both. The results are the existing overlapping in income taxes, in business taxes, in death duties, and in excises like the taxes on gasoline, on tobacco, on transactions, and the like. The crying need of the future is a coördination of our revenue system whereby some semblance of order may be introduced into the fast-growing fiscal chaos, and as a result of which due consideration may be paid not only to the total burden on the taxpayer but also to the respective claims of State and federal finance.

The third point in any estimate of our future fiscal system is the difficulty into which we have fallen because of the existence of tax-exempt securities. When the system first developed, it was of little fiscal consequence. But now, with over thirty billion dollars of outstanding tax-exempt securities, the situation is full of menace. Reciprocal tax exemption seems likely to nullify the advantages ascribable to a satisfactory federal income tax or an adequate State bank or corporation tax. Under a system of strictly proportional taxation the tax on such securities might well be deemed prepaid. But in the face of progressive taxation and the impossibility of knowing in advance into which bracket the holdings will fall, the exemption, no longer reflected in the higher market value, becomes a distinct immunity, frustrating to this extent the entire scheme of graduation. The removal of this anomaly is a condition precedent to a successful functioning of a well-considered tax system.

25

The formulation of a plan to function under what we may hope will be the normal conditions of the next four or five years is therefore not so simple as may appear at first blush. To judge from present indications the total expenditures of the nation through its various governmental agencies will amount to some fourteen or fifteen billion dollars, of which about one-third will be ascribable to the federal government. Of the nine or ten billions spent in the States the chief reliance must continue to be the old general property tax, which is fast changing into a semi-personal tax on real estate. The mounting burden on the landowner, which is in the larger cities partly shifted to the tenant and partly amortized by a slower appreciation of land values, can be in a measure relieved by a resort to other revenues, like a share in the coördinated system of income, business, inheritance, gasoline, and other indirect taxes. This raises the question as to how much can be expected from such a series of coördinated taxes. It is obviously neither necessary nor practicable to attempt exact figures. What is important in framing a program is to show the general trend. Precise estimates depend not only on the rates selected but on the oscillations in economic life.

Using then only very rough and general figures, we may begin with the income tax. The yield of the federal individual income tax has varied from three-quarters to over one and one-quarter billion dollars. If we take the year 1928 as an indication of prosperity coupled with moderate rates, and if we add the State income taxes, it is probable that we may expect under normal conditions a yield of roughly one and one-half billions from this source. The corporate income tax has yielded

26

between one and one and one-quarter billions. If we add to this the corporation and business taxes in the States, we may again expect with substantially existing rates a yield of perhaps two billions. From a coördinated income tax we may therefore anticipate under normal conditions and moderate rates about three and one-half billions. This is, of course, only a very small proportion of the total social income.

With the inheritance tax or death duties we enter a far more controverted field. The yield of the estate tax has been exceedingly low, partly because of loopholes in the law, partly because of the large rebate to the States. It is worthy of note, however, that the net taxable estates have gradually increased to about two and one-half billion dollars. This is a very low figure, due in part to the excessive exemptions. In England, with one-third of the population and a very much smaller total wealth, the net taxable estates were actually greater than with us. In 1931 the British revenues from death duties was over $400,000,000 as compared with about $1,600,000,000 from income tax. A very much lower maximum rate than in Great Britain would easily yield with us in normal times a revenue of a half-billion dollars. This would mean less than a sixth of the income tax instead of a quarter as in Great Britain. And if the loopholes in our law were stopped up, and the exemption were made generous instead of excessive, the burden would be relatively inconspicuous.

Coming to the other revenues, we could easily count on a half-billion dollars each from customs and tobacco, a billion from gasoline, and a billion from a self-supporting postal service, making a total coördinated revenue of six and one-half billion dollars. If prohibition were abolished and liquor taxes reinstituted, there is little doubt that there would be a further yield of about one and one-half billions. The net result would be a coördinated revenue of eight billion dollars, leaving for the local property tax almost six or seven billions. Inasmuch as the federal government ought to need only about five billions, three billions would be available for the States, with a reasonably substantial reduction of the burden of the local property tax.

If, on the other hand, we persist in deliberately renouncing the easily collectible liquor tax, we should have to make good the difference by a multiplicity of excises, by a substantial increase of the gasoline tax, or by a rise in the rates of both income and inheritance taxes. The first of these choices may be rejected as undesirable. The choice between the other two will depend largely upon the preference that may be assigned to the relative merits of the benefit and the ability theory in taxation. But there will also remain a consideration of the point at which the advantages of a more equitable distribution of wealth are outweighed by a possible retardation in the process of accumulation. In any event the potential resources of the country are so gigantic that we may face with equanimity a fiscal future which, if informed with intelligence and a prudent regard for the economic and social consequences of taxation, will unite ample revenue with moderate and fairly apportioned burdens.

28

LEO WOLMAN

is professor of economics in Columbia University. As the representative of Governor Roosevelt he was chairman of the Interstate Commission on Unemployment Insurance. He participated, as director of the research department of the Amalgamated Clothing Workers, in drafting and organizing the well-known plan of unemployment insurance which has been in operation in the men's clothing industry of Chicago since 1923. He has written extensively on the economic aspects of unemployment and unemployment insurance and, in 1930, published a study of the relation between unemployment and public works entitled "The Planning and Control of Public Works."

Unemployment Insurance

THE WORLD has now had more than twenty years of experience with many kinds of unemployment insurance. The rise and development of this latest form of social insurance has taken place under the unusual conditions of universal war-time inflation and boom, followed by successive periods of the most drastic economic and financial readjustment of which we have any record. Certainly, so far as the period since 1920 in Europe is concerned, it is fair enough to say that unemployment-insurance plans could not have encountered more difficult problems than those existing during the decade of the twenties. Europe, therefore—and in particular England and Germany—has served as a laboratory for the rest of the world and has managed somehow to handle unemployment in a new and more effective way at a time when unemployment has been abnormal both in volume and duration.

As a result of this experience no country need any longer remain in the dark concerning the important features of workable unemployment insurance and the paths which reform in existing plans and in future experiments must take. The emissaries from President Hoover recently sent to Europe for the study of foreign difficulties, wherever their facts were accurate, reported nothing that had not been known for some time by all students of the problem. And even the disclosures of the last Commission of Inquiry under the MacDonald Labor Government could not possibly have surprised any one at all close to the English plan and familiar with current reports of the Ministry of Labor and the findings of earlier investigations by parliamentary committees.

Since it is only sensible to learn from experience, it is best to begin this discussion with a brief appraisal of the benefits and demerits of the English scheme, which has had the longest history and which has been constantly in the public eye.

Viewed simply as a source of unemployment relief, the English system of insurance has been an unprecedented achievement. Largely, if not exclusively, as a result of the unemployment insurance, unemployed English workingmen have been able to maintain their standard of living. After more than ten years of general depression in the majority of industries, and virtual stagnation in the rest, it is the consensus of informed opinion that poverty in England has been reduced and that average standards of life are higher than they were before the war. Compulsory insurance, on a national scale, has proved administratively practicable. The vast machinery for the collection of contributions and the distribution of benefits, covering 12,000,000 insured workers and thousands of businesses, and charged with the operation of a national system of employment exchanges, has been administered with rare skill, honesty, and intelligence. The risk of unemployment has been, in the main, fairly and objectively defined. And the grosser manifestations of malingering have never been regarded as a serious problem by either the advocates or opponents of the insurance system.

At the same time the insurance plan has suffered from the disability of being unable to balance its budgets without large and mounting subsidies from the government. This condition, in turn, is the direct and inevitable consequence of the persistence in England of unprecedented unemployment not alone in any single year but during each of the years from 1921 to the present. The prevalence of an unemployment rate rarely dropping below 10 per cent and often exceeding 20 per cent of the working population, with unusually long spells of idleness for thousands of workingmen, completely upset the actuarial calculations on which the original structure of rates of premiums and benefits was based. To continue to regard the English arrangement as an insurance scheme, only two possible courses of action were open to its administration—first, a radical revision of both premiums and benefits, with a view to making the plan self-supporting, and, second, the removal from under the insurance plan of all those who had technically and legally exhausted their right to insurance benefits because they had been forced by lack of work to cease all contributions into the unemployment fund. Whatever the reason, successive English governments failed to take either course, and the insurance fund fell deeper and deeper into debt. It is true, of course, that the ineligible unemployed might anyhow have been supported by the public treasury, but they would then not have been a burden on the insurance fund and their support would have been treated as a straightforward problem in public relief.

Aside from this obvious and generally admitted difficulty, which the present English government has recently taken steps to remove, other important criticisms of the English system are more debatable. The English plan, as every one knows, provides for the pooling of all unemployment premiums. The contributions by both the stable and unstable industries, therefore, flow into the same national unemployment fund, and during the kind of depression England has had since 1920, the industries with low unemployment rates have to all intents and purposes been subsidizing the more depressed industries, like coal, textiles, and shipbuilding. Those who regard unemployment as a national problem, uncontrollable by single industries, and unemployment insurance as almost exclusively a relief measure, still strongly favor the English method. Critics like Sir William Beveridge, on the other hand, believe the single pool to be the source of many evils, since it diffuses the responsibility for unemployment and imposes no effective obligation on individual employers and industries to handle their own unemployment problems. The issue here raised is one of great theoretical and practical importance, involving consideration of the preventive and relief features of unemployment insurance. But, disregarding this larger question for the moment, the fact

32

remains that the graver problems of English unemployment might in the long run have been more successfully managed through the establishment of insurance plans limited certainly to single industries and perhaps to single firms.

The charge that unemployment insurance has restricted the mobility of labor, and hence retarded inevitable adjustments in industry, is even more open to difference of opinion. The measurable facts disclose considerable mobility within the English labor market, the expansion of industry into new areas, and the rise of "new" industries. The facts are, however, not conclusive; nor can they be made so. Where unemployment is the result of a multitude of the most obscure economic forces, it is plainly impossible to assign the proper weight to any one of them. It is, nevertheless, important to realize that unemployment insurance, administered poorly and on unsound principles, can effectively block the free movement of labor and that, to the extent to which it does immobilize labor, it may do a great deal of harm, not only to industry, but to the beneficiaries of insurance as well. For any form of insurance which tends to prolong unemployment and to increase the numbers unemployed thereby seriously impairs the benefits it affords through the payment of unemployment relief.

If, then, the sponsors of proposed schemes of unemployment insurance hope to secure the solvency of unemployment funds, to achieve a fair balance between the preventive and relief features of the system, and to preserve flexibility in industrial operations, scrutiny of the history of England's insurance furnishes the ex-

33

perience from which the appropriate standards of legislation and administration can be obtained. While the European systems and the few American plans of unemployment insurance differ substantially in many details from the English, they all show evidence of creating much the same type of problems.

The most effective and perhaps the only safeguard of solvency is a clear and strict limitation of the right to benefit. This limitation is exercised by the application of rules fixing the ratio between the amounts of benefits paid to any unemployed person and the number of his contributions into the unemployment fund. In extreme cases the limitation may be extended to provide for the cessation of all benefits once the unemployment fund has fallen to a specified amount. These provisions are, of course, analogous to the terms of all other insurance contracts. In life insurance, for example, the face value of a policy varies directly with the amount of the premium, and the value of the policy is adjusted when the terms of the contract are changed by the failure of the policy-holder to pay his premiums. If life and other insurance companies undertook to distribute benefits in accordance with need, without reference to their premium receipts, they would all shortly become insolvent.

In the administration of unemployment insurance, the enforcement of such limitations would unquestionably work great hardship on many unemployed. In all countries and at all times there are a varying number of unemployed who are in no position to pay unemployment premiums either because they can find no jobs or because they are unemployable. How large this num-

34

ber is in the United States there is no way of knowing. But it is a fair guess that the unemployables and the long-time unemployed are a small proportion of the total number out of work in both normal and abnormal times. In England, where permanent unemployment is believed to be quite general, the facts do not support the prevailing view. "More or less continuous unemployment," a recent government report states, "is confined to a very small section of the insured population which cannot include more than 100,000 men and 3,000 women. This group represents the maximum size of the 'standing army' of the unemployed. The number of those who have had no unemployment is at least thirty times as large. Betweeen these two extremes there is a group, about one and one half times as numerous as the other two combined, and including about 5,500,000 men and 1,700,000 women, among whom employment and unemployment are intermittent. In this group the degree of unemployment is not uniform. Among at least half the group unemployment is almost negligible, and it becomes serious among only about 10 per cent." If these figures are even roughly applicable to the American situation, as they probably are, they show that a limited plan of unemployment insurance, covering more than 75 per cent of the workers of the country, could have been kept solvent even during the post-war years.

It follows from this exhibit as well as from our general knowledge of unemployment that chronic unemployment is not properly insurable. The several hundred thousand unemployed coal miners, who may never again find anything like full employment under decent conditions in the soft-coal industry, cannot be kept in-

35

definitely insured without exhausting the resources of
an unemployment fund and thus hastening its insolvency. Because such employees in sick or declining industries face long periods of total unemployment, for
which there is no immediate remedy, everything should
be done through organized public relief and the provision of facilities for vocational guidance and industrial
training to promote mobility and the absorption of surplus labor into other industries. By thus classifying the
unemployed into those who may hope to find a reasonable amount of employment in an industry and those
who can look forward to only the most intermittent and
irregular employment, and by adjusting the methods
of handling the problem to the peculiar needs of each
group, unemployment-insurance principles and administrative procedure are already taking the first step in
what is destined to become a vast elaboration of the
machinery of unemployment relief and prevention.

Recognition of the necessity for unemployment classification as an indispensable element in unemployment
insurance accounts for the character of the Wisconsin
unemployment-reserve law and for the type of plan
recommended by the Interstate Commission on Unemployment Insurance. The Wisconsin system undertakes
primarily to meet the problem of the permanent or
regular employee. From a fund, amounting to 2 per
cent of the weekly pay roll, such employees will receive
moderate benefits during limited periods of unemployment. While highly irregular and casual employees are
also eligible to benefits under this plan, their total possible benefits are bound to be too small to do them
much good. For them the community and industry will

be forced to devise further provisions suitable for the treatment of the various types of chronic unemployment.

Limitation of the right to benefit as a means of insuring the solvency of unemployment funds and of classifying the unemployed does not, however, touch the equally important problem involved in making unemployment benefits available when they are most needed. If we may judge by universal experience, we may safely assume that no plan of unemployment insurance so far devised can possibly yield benefits for all types of unemployment. The ordinary workingman with a job in an insured industry is normally exposed to one or all of several forms of unemployment—the unemployment due to seasonal slackness, the loss of job due to the introduction of machinery, and the prolonged idleness associated with general industrial depression. Unless, in the circumstances, provision is specifically made for each of these contingencies, workingmen may find, as they often have, that they have exhausted their right to benefit at a time when they are most sorely in need of unemployment relief.

For this condition there is obviously no simple solution. But attack on the problem consists in arriving at a clean-cut decision as to the purpose of an unemployment-insurance plan. In the early history of nearly all unemployment insurance, no distinction was made between the many types of unemployment, and, consequently, the liberal payment of benefits for seasonal unemployment, for instance, left the fund in many cases with totally inadequate resources either at the beginning or during the early stages of a severe business decline.

37

With the accumulation of experience it has become clear that the wise policy is to lay aside as much as possible against the extraordinary upheavals of industry and to make only the most moderate compensation for the normal unemployment experienced in good times. Accordingly, in considering the revision of the unemployment-insurance rules in one seasonal industry, it has now been proposed that the waiting period—the period which elapses between the beginning of unemployment and the first payment of benefit—should be extended from one to three weeks a season or six weeks a year. The effect of this rule is to regard forty-six weeks as a normal year's employment in this industry. If such a rule had been in force in the six years preceding this depression, the insured workingman would have received smaller benefits before 1930; but, from the larger insurance reserves unemployed workmen would have received much greater benefits during the past two and a half years, the period of most severe unemployment.

The use of unemployment insurance as a method for the prevention of unemployment or the reduction in its amount is still more a matter of theory than of practical experience. On the failure of the English plan to encourage prevention, there seems to be in this country almost general agreement; and the English failure in this respect is usually attributed to the method of the national unemployment pool. Accordingly, American proposals, by analogy with the terms of our workmen's compensation acts, either provide for insurance by industry and the adjustment of the premiums of individual employers within each industry to their employment records, or they provide outright insurance by individual firms. The Wisconsin law is of the latter type. By its terms, each firm is required by law to set up its own unemployment reserve into which it contributes 2 per cent of its weekly pay roll. Out of this reserve the firm pays benefits for a limited period of time and under specified conditions to its unemployed workingmen. Where, however, the reserve reaches indicated amounts, the firm may either reduce its current contributions or, where the reserve has mounted still higher, may discontinue payments altogether. The payment of premiums is not again resumed until the reserves have been reduced by amounts also specified in the law. By thus imposing responsibility for the unemployment of his work force directly upon each employer and by offering him financial incentives to regularize employment, it is hoped to achieve progress in the prevention of unemployment.

How effective such incentives will be can be learned only from experience. If we may judge by the degree of employment irregularity in this country and by the intensity of the business depressions of the past, it is doubtful that any considerable stabilization can be achieved through unemployment insurance alone. Serious attempts to control business during the boom, on the theory that control then exercised will mitigate the severity of the next collapse, are less likely to be made through the instrumentality of insurance than by the regulation of the operations of banking and investment. Coupled with such control it may then be entirely feasible and sound to extend existing unemployment-insurance arrangements by imposing a substantial tax on the expansion of pay rolls and by using the proceeds of this tax not alone for the payment of ordinary unemployment benefits but, more especially, for the provision of adequate separation or discharge wages.

Unemployment insurance of the future, then, is bound to assume a variety of forms. All forms should involve the careful definition of the risk of unemployment and strict limitations on the right to benefit. The details of each insurance system will be in large part determined by its purpose. Where the essential purpose of the plan is the regularization of employment, it will provide moderate benefits for the unemployed and financial incentives to the employer. In such plans premiums into the unemployment reserves will be necessarily paid by the employer alone. The reserves, moreover, designed to mitigate the effects of chronic irregularities of employment among regular employees will be of little help in long spells of unemployment.

As a source of relief against the unemployment of business depressions, unemployment funds must be assured a substantial period of accumulation. They must also be very large in amount. For the accumulation of funds of this nature, premium should be paid by both employers and employees and their combined premium should not be less than 3 per cent of the total pay roll. These funds, moreover, if they are to yield adequate benefits during prolonged depressions without the assistance of public subsidy should not be drawn upon heavily in times of normal business. Depression reserves of this kind must be administered as strictly insurance funds and must be protected against unpredictable and excessive demands for benefits by the device of a long waiting period, by the enforcement of all restrictions on the right to benefit, and by the elimination from the scheme of all unemployed who are unable to satisfy statutory requirements.

These, in bare outline, are the principles which, in my judgment, should guide American experiments in unemployment insurance. At the best, insurance can in no sense be regarded as a solution of the unemployment problem. It is at the same time an effort toward greater stabilization of employment and the more decent and constructive handling of unemployment relief. Under the most favorable conditions, also, it will be rare that unemployment-insurance systems, however universal and compulsory, will be in a position to furnish adequate relief to all of the unemployed. There will for some time remain, in normal as well as in depression times, a residuum of unemployed unable to find jobs and ineligible to insurance benefits unless the principles of sound insurance practice are violated. The support and industrial rehabilitation of these unemployed, and the task of returning them to industry, are the proper and sole functions of the State, to be financed not out of insurance funds but out of the income from taxation.

CLARENCE S. STEIN

*is a New York architect and community planner. He was for-
merly chairman of the Commission of Housing and Regional
Planning of New York State.*

Housing and Common Sense

THERE is a fairy story about housing that all Ameri-
cans like to believe. It tells us that any American
of sound character and industrious habits can provide
himself with "the house of his heart's desire." The picture of that fairy-story dwelling is exhibited in various
forms in those home journals and other magazines that
carry advertisements of all the mechanical gadgets
which constitute the glory of that house. It has all the
pretension of a great mansion and the picturesque cute-
ness of a little cottage. It is always displayed in a spaci-
ous garden, free of surrounding buildings, yet it is served
by all the conveniences of modern urban civilization.

Now the hard facts are quite different from the fairy
story. It is only the man with plenty of money who can
have his house planned and built to meet his needs and
can place it so as to secure quiet and privacy. Private
enterprise does supply homes for this very limited part
of the population. Housing for the well-to-do is a good
business, but housing for two-thirds of our citizens is
nobody's business. The cost of habitation is so disproportionate to their incomes that most people cannot af-
ford new houses. They are forced to live in dwellings
left over from another and different age, most of which
are now far below American standards of decency and
sanitation. And most of the houses built during the last

42

ten years are no better than the old. They are little more than decorated wooden boxes crowded and shouldered by an army of other wooden boxes. They lack all the elementary needs of decent dwellings: sound construction, adequate sunlight, ventilation, privacy, and surroundings of natural green. They have no architectural sincerity; they are false and artificial settings for a moving-picture life. They ape the customs of a past age instead of meeting the needs of the present.

In spite of the unprecedented progress in all other great industries, the standard of house construction during the past decade has been lower than before the war. Progress there has been, but mainly in such mechanical accessories as bathroom, kitchen, and furnace fittings that are made and assembled in factories. The shell itself—that portion of the house that is put together by labor on the job—shows no technical progress. Problems of insulation against heat and cold and sound and of fire resistance have been generally left unsolved. Most of our houses are still made of wood in spite of the danger of fire and rapid deterioration. Compared with earlier periods, the construction has been slovenly—poor materials badly put together. A large part of it is the slipshod work of ignorant or irresponsible jerry-builders.

The quality of housing—and in part its cost—is due to the fact that the building industry is organized on a retail basis. Mass production we have in and near our large cities, where the greater part of the houses are produced by wholesale. But the antiquated methods of the days when houses were built one by one for individual owners persist. As a result, housing is our one large industry that has been practically unaffected by the great decade of industrial standardization and mechanization.

Most of the houses built during the last ten years were badly placed because they were planned to fit deep narrow lots rather than the needs of growing human beings who require sunlight and air and the sight of natural green. They have been placed without any regard to the best use of the site or the preservation of open spaces. Similar houses have been arranged in endless lines, like soldiers on parade—miles of identical, free-standing houses, with no individuality and no privacy. Traditional systems of land subdivision, which bear no relation to actual use, like the typical municipal regulations, lead to the building of monotonous rows, and make it practically impossible to group houses so as to secure beauty or to obtain the maximum advantages of vista and privacy.

In the motor age our municipalities have continued to repeat highway and street layouts patterned for the days of the buggy. All the requirements of living have changed, but the framework of our cities remains the same. In fact, they are extended endlessly according to obsolete and wasteful methods in spite of the apparent need of new types of city planning to meet the requirements of the use of the automobile and the growing demand for peaceful escape from the dangers, noises, and odors of traffic highways.

Vast areas of land have been taken out of productive use for farming long before they were needed for housing. They have been subdivided into small lots and marketed by super-sales methods that add vastly to the cost of the land to the ultimate owner. More lots have

44

been sold in these last ten years than can be used for decades—perhaps a century. Much of the land will lie useless for long periods while the owners' costs are inflated by payments for interest on investments, taxes, and assessments for roads, and public utilities. Vast lengths of this expensive municipal equipment—highways, sewers, water supplies, as well as gas mains, telephones, and electric wires—are but partially used as one building after another is erected. The houses that are built fit badly in their narrow lots. But the mold of the future development of this portion of the city has been fixed by street layouts and subdivisions that are in great part already obsolete. Under our present procedure the pattern can be changed, the mold broken, only at vast expense and much labor by repurchase of individual lots.

Subdivisions have been located in accordance with the whim of the speculator rather than as required by a sound economic development of the community or the region of which they form a part. As a result, there is a chaotic relation between the location of industry and the home of workers. Municipalities have been put to vast expense—or more often have borrowed on the future—for transportation systems to connect the two.

A large part of the housing has been recklessly financed. The lending institutions hold the key position in the house-building industry. It is their loans that make construction possible. It is their final say which decides what houses shall be built. In short, they have been the real leaders in this chaotic industry. Loans have often been made without proper consideration of the quality of construction, the ability and integrity of the

45

builder, the financial ability of the purchasers to meet all costs of upkeep, future assessments, and taxes, or the future character of the neighborhood as affecting the value of the house.

The causes of our past failures are not far to seek. Basically there are two. First, housing is carried on as speculation rather than investment. Second, housing is looked upon as purely a private affair rather than a public function. The American concept of building a house is a survival of the days when each man could provide his own home in his own way. In the pioneer days the individual could and did build his own home and supply its equipment on a purely individualistic basis. But with the development of the complications of modern urban life all this has changed. Much that we now consider essential to the house, such as good highways, sidewalks, water mains, sewers, telephones, gas and electricity, cannot be the individual's affair. It is a public matter, installed by the municipality or as a public utility. Parks, schools, transportation, and other facilities which make a neighborhood of houses desirable are also supplied at the expense of the city. The city's investment in housing is great. It cannot protect that investment under our present system of uncontrolled development of the city's growth for speculative gain.

The extravagant type of streets and utilities planned for the newer sections of our cities cannot be supported by those willing to occupy the cheap, free-standing houses with which these sections have been covered. Their cost must in part be borne by other parts of the city. The transportation lines and highways which feed

46

these sections must also be subsidized. Meanwhile, streets, utilities, and the protection of the older blighted areas which have been in large part vacated in the outward growth of these same cities must also be carried at a loss. The uncontrolled growth of our urban regions is one of the factors that are leading all our big cities toward bankruptcy. It is its relation to their fiscal rather than to their social success or failure that will ultimately force our municipalities to accept housing as a public utility.

Although we think in terms of the pioneer—of the individual building his own house—the truth is that most dwellings are produced not for use but as speculation. This is the key to most of our housing difficulties. Houses are built to sell, and so it is mainly on the outward appearance rather than the essential structure that the builder's money is spent. He is not interested in supplying a need; he wants to make a profit. He would rather employ a clever salesman than a competent plumber, an honest carpenter, or an efficient architect. He puts very little real money into the operation. What he cannot borrow he owes to his subcontractors. He gets out as quickly as possible and moves on to speculate with the future development of some other section of the city.

Meanwhile, the house buyer who thought he had made an investment discovers he has gambled away his economic freedom. The fairy-story house he bought is only skin deep. The ownership of a home which according to the propaganda was to have made him a better citizen has merely robbed him of his freedom of movement. The "Own your own home" campaigns have en-

47

couraged many to buy who never should have done so
—and never would have done so if they really had un-
derstood what they were getting into. The enormous
number of foreclosures of mortgages in 1931 illustrates
this point. The purchaser has been chained to a house
that was ill fitted to his needs in the beginning, and
was so badly built and so badly placed that it will be
worthless long before the mortgages have been paid and
the building really belongs to him. Deterioration of
house or obsolescence of neighborhood wipes out his
life's savings and one-quarter of his earnings for the
better part of his working years. If houses were built
as an investment instead of a speculation they would be
constructed so that their structural life would be safe
during the period in which the investment was being
paid off. The neighborhood would be planned, built,
and restricted so as to protect their value.

The speculative basis of housing is responsible not
only for deterioration of buildings and neighborhood,
but also for most of the wasteful and useless processes
which make houses too expensive for most families.
These include the waste of pyramiding land costs by
premature land subdivision and sales; the waste in high-
pressure salesmanship; the waste of partially used public
improvements; the waste of bad planning; and the
waste of small-scale construction methods. But the waste
that costs the buyer or the renter of house or apartment
most is that which comes from exorbitant charges for
the use of money. It is because housing is a speculative
business rather than a sound investment that its financing
is so expensive. The actual annual costs for the use of
money are generally in excess of 9 per cent. If the rate

48

of financing were cut one-third, from 9 per cent to 6 per cent, rents could be cut about one-fifth.

Now if housing were a good and a safe investment, there would be no reason why the charges for the use of money should be higher than the market rates. There is no safer investment than a soundly constructed house in a properly planned and organized neighborhood. It is good for thirty years or more, and rental charges could be reduced not only by decreased rate of interest, but also by decreased amortization charges. Money at 4½ per cent instead of 9 would mean that a four-room apartment that rents for $60 could be rented for $42.

It is apparent that the way to decent housing and communities and to economic housing is the same. If we could forget the fairy stories about housing and would use a little common sense, we would scrap most of our present housing methods and create new processes and new agencies. We would accept as a basis for our program of the future:

1. Housing as an investment rather than a speculation.

2. Housing as a public service rather than an individual function.

Such a realistic program for the future would presuppose:

1. *No more subdivisions of land* before actual planning and building of homes.

2. *No more planning or building of houses* as single, unrelated units within urban areas.

3. *No more construction* by irresponsible, unskilled, small-scale builders.

49

Now let me put a program for the future on a positive rather than a negative basis. Roughly it is:

1. *Plan and build communities, not unrelated individual houses.* Plan every house as an integrated and related part of the whole town and more particularly of the neighborhood. The neighborhood should be the minimum unit of design. These communities should be created to meet the requirements of a new age—the age of the motor and increased leisure. They should be built spaciously around great parks. They should offer both the conveniences of this machine age and an escape from its nuisances and dangers.

2. *Build these neighborhood communities as a single operation or a series of related large-scale operations* under the guidance of trained technicians working as an organized group. Thus we can secure towns fitted not only to our modern needs but, what is quite as important, to our pocketbooks.

3. *Relate the location of these communities to the most desirable economic and social development of the city and region.* We shall thus secure better environment for living and a saner relation of housing to work and recreation places. At the same time we shall vastly decrease the cost of housing and particularly the accessory governmental costs of roads, utilities, and transportation. We may even escape municipal bankruptcy.

4. *Reorganize the house-building industry* as a modern and efficient large-scale industry.

5. *Put land for housing purposes under government control.* Thus do away with premature land subdivision and turn land directly from productive farm use to the

50

maximum productive use for housing. Every farsighted municipality should purchase surrounding rural land and hold it out of use for housing until it is really needed—forever, if possible. It should also—for the social good of its citizens and its own economic salvation —take over the vast rotting or blighted areas both in the older sections and in those newer regions in which the cancerous signs of blight are beginning to appear. This will require a new type of condemnation law that will give the government a chance to take land on a fair basis of actual value.

6. *Finance housing on an investment instead of a speculative basis.* Large-scale operation would simplify housing financing and help to safeguard investments. It spreads the risks instead of concentrating them as do individual loans. Its scale and the homogeneous character it gives a neighborhood preserve the values for a much longer time than does our present method. Because the risk is decreased, loans on a larger percentage of value, longer periods of amortization, and a smaller return on money are possible. On the basis of a complete new set-up, substantial amounts of capital seeking permanent investment would be drawn into housing, for housing built according to the program outlined above would be one of the safest and soundest investments. It therefore should command money at the lowest market rate of interest. Its securities would market as readily as do the bonds of the Port Authority if each house-building operation had behind it the supervision and the approval of governmental agencies, such as the New York State Housing Board. As a result, instead of housing one-third of our population in the haphazard, wasteful, and

unsatisfactory method of the past, it would be possible to produce on a sound business basis decent homes for perhaps two-thirds of our urban population.

There will still remain a great many workers whose wages are too low to pay for new dwellings no matter how efficiently and economically they are produced. They must be housed not partially, as at present, but entirely, as a public service. In the past public-spirited citizens and foundations have attempted to care for the housing of the poor. Their work stands head and shoulders above most of the speculative developments. They have blazed the way in creating neighborhoods of permanent value as a result of unified planning, coördinated building, and sane regulations. Their investments have in most cases been safeguarded by the character of their work.

Housing for the lower income groups must become a direct governmental service—in my opinion a service far more important than the building of roads, utilities, transportation, even more important than schools. Why continue to dodge the problem? Inadequate incomes never will pay for adequate homes. We shall have decent communities for the vast mass of the population only when our cities—houses and all—are financed and built as public services. This means a vast amount of public credit for long terms and at low rates—rates as low as that at which the government can borrow, and even lower for the very poor. This does not necessarily mean an actual loss to the government. Certainly the loss to the city or State will not be so great as that which municipalities now suffer because of our present wasteful methods of city and housing development.

E. G. NOURSE

is Director of the Institute of Economics of the Brookings Institution at Washington, and was formerly professor of Agricultural Economics at Iowa State College.

Can the American Farm Be Saved?

MOST of us are getting restive now that the depression is stretching out beyond the period that expounders of business cycles had led us to expect. During the first year we were buoyed up by prognostications of a "minor cycle" and hopes of early recovery. As the second year wore on we thought we were fulfilling any probable requirement of expiation. But now that we are well into the third year of depression, with most of our friends very bearish about the future, we insist that something drastic be done.

Since the troubles of agriculture began so far back as 1920, many people are moved to advocate the most extreme measures to deal with rural problems. Are not the farmers, after eleven full years of suffering, entitled to priority in the nation's program of economic recovery? Doubtless. But unfortunately agriculture is not the logical place to begin with our reconstruction program. The major planks in any realistic platform of economic rehabilitation relate to public and private finance and to the quickening of industrial activity and the revival of commercial exchange. Agricultural prosperity will follow naturally in the wake of any such general trade revival, whereas no amount of specific tinkering with agriculture can initiate a general price recovery.

53

On the other hand, there are several definite threats to agriculture in the present situation if it is allowed to drift. These harmful influences might still further impair the position of agriculture and cause it to contribute to a yet deeper demoralization of the whole business situation. Or, if general recession were checked at this point, they would militate seriously against the farmer's efforts to secure a satisfactory economic position for himself during the period of recovery. These difficulties center chiefly around the questions of ownership of the farm plant, access to land for agricultural use, and charges on land. Any sane agricultural program at the present time should bear three general injunctions in mind.

1. Don't take the farmer's land away from him.

2. Don't tax him to death.

3. Don't leave submarginal areas to private exploitation.

The depression has now advanced to that acute stage where people on every hand—bankers, business men, farmers—have been losing control of their productive properties simply because they are forced into a position of technical insolvency by reason of the marking down of their assets through distress selling in a market already clogged with previous distress sales. If we allow this process to continue of its own momentum it will result in devaluing everything by putting it simultaneously on the auction block. There is nothing to be gained and much to be lost by forcing farms out of the hands of those to whom they are a home and a career and forcing them into the hands of those to whom they are a burden and expense and in whose hands they suffer deterioration of productivity.

In the early twenties I advised Iowa farmers to let farms bought during the boom go back to the sellers or mortgagees and to avail themselves of bankruptcy proceedings rather freely as a means of shifting to other parts of society a burden which had fallen on their shoulders, not through any fault of their own so much as through the operation of a far-flung combination of social forces. Most of them tried to hang on, and there was a good deal of stretching of credit to enable them to do so in order to protect an inflated capitalization. Most of those who bought land at "war prices" have by now given up their farms and accepted the loss of much or all of the family's savings. But many farmers still hold farms inherited from the previous generation or bought at pre-boom prices. As the years of mounting costs and shrinking returns have succeeded one another, they have put new mortgages on these farms or added to old ones. And they have had to put all that they could sweat out of themselves and their families into holding their mortgaged acres. It would be a cruel injustice to force them out at this late stage of the price decline. Not only this: to do so would further disrupt our agriculture.

We should have a general moratorium on foreclosures and forced sales until we can see on what price level agricultural commodities and farm lands are going to stabilize themselves. The action of Congress in putting an additional $125,000,000 into the Federal Farm Loan system will help materially toward this end. Such stabilization as results from the Reconstruction Finance Corporation is another step in the right direction, even though belated. These measures should be amplified by every other possible means of carrying out the same policy. But we ought to go farther than this. Mortgage obligations should be scaled down to the actual earning value which agricultural lands will have during the working lifetime of the present generation as nearly as this can be estimated. And methods of estimating should be conservative.

Such a procedure would be an innovation in the field of farm finance. But it is an old story in corporation finance. When security holders find that a company has been capitalized far beyond its actual earning power and any reasonable prospect of future earnings, they frequently deem it expedient to resort to constructive reorganization rather than destructive liquidation. Preferred stocks are drastically pruned and bonds scaled down even without extinguishing the shareholder's interest. Such a course is followed where and because there seems to be prospect of permanent income through the continuation of existing operative arrangements, and where labor and management can be paid only if fixed charges are substantially reduced.

A similar situation obtains today over a large part of our agricultural industry. Where farms are foreclosed in any considerable numbers, the quondam mortgagee, as new owner, finds himself hard put to it to continue the lands in even such productivity as they had before, while the dispossessed owner often finds it difficult to secure employment which will contribute as much to the family living as he could get from the old farm, unprosperous though it was. We need to make some drastic revision of the claims upon farm income as between capitalists and workers.

However lamentable the losses which our farmers have been suffering, they are infinitely less disruptive of the nation's economic well-being than it would be to drive the farm families off the hundreds of thousands of farms where they are in arrears on mortgage obligations. The loss would be less also than leaving these families in possession only on condition that arrears of interest accumulate and compound on a principal sum in excess of present value and prospective earning power. This preserves nominal ownership at the cost of future decades or generations of work, exploited to support a war-time capitalization. The most wholesome result all around will come from realistically facing revaluation in the light of changed conditions.

As for taxation, practically every one who has studied the matter agrees that the antiquated general property tax puts an undue burden on agriculture. This disparity is inordinately magnified with the growth of the total tax load. It was bad enough in the days of the district schools and mud roads, but with the attempt to bring rural standards of living up measurably close to those of the town it has become intolerable. The urban cynic answers that the rural sections should be content with the little red schoolhouse or stop squawking about the expense of more modern school advantages. This quite overlooks the fact that the rural sections, which average a lower per capita income than the rest of the country, have to provide the most of schooling—not to mention the birth and rearing—of a larger quota of children. After living in the country during their dependent

57

childhood they move to town to spend their productive adult years. The road problem is somewhat similar. Automobile highways were built in response to urban demand, and the profits from their construction have practically all gone to the city, but a disproportionate amount of their cost has been assessed upon abutting farm property. With mounting school and road taxes, the farmer's bill has been rising to $400, $600, and $800 on a quarter-section farm from which it has become increasingly difficult, not to say impossible, to get a $1,500 or $2,000 annual income. In poorer sections it may be $100 of tax out of $600 or $800 of income. Here the pressure is even more severe.

This problem cannot soundly be met by the scaling down of these services. Country schools are still, on the average, much behind even village schools. A large percentage of our farmers are still relatively isolated on roads impassable for periods of weeks or months. And adequate hospitalization and even moderate public-health service are yet to be provided. The cost must be socialized through shifting the burden to State and national budgets, putting taxes largely on an income basis, the more courageous use of death duties, and the use of registration and gasoline taxes for support of the road system.

In one direction, however, there is an excellent prospect of reducing the cost of local government. We still maintain an elaborate system of horse-and-buggy counties in an automobile age. No one but a blind man could spend an afternoon in a rural county courthouse without being aware that rural counties as a whole are maintaining facilities and personnel two, four, or six times those

58

that would be required for the adequate performance
of the service on the basis of full-time work for the
necessary functionaries. Vested interest in the village
and political conservatism on the farms make the task
of pruning off this excess growth a difficult one. But it
presents an outstanding opportunity for economy without sacrifice of social service—the chance to clip a coupon
on our investment in hard roads.

A third suggestion for safeguarding the farmer's economic position concerns land policy. We hear a storm
of protest about overproduction, the "surplus problem,"
wholesale reversion of lands, and the cost and inade-
quacy of public services in thinly settled regions. It is
high time that we woke up to the fact that these questions run back largely to the basic problem of land
utilization, and that the troubles can be very greatly
ameliorated even though not entirely cured by the
formulation and enforcement of a new and enlightened
land policy.

For three hundred years we have sought to encourage and stimulate the maximum private settlement
and ownership of our land area, with unregulated private business enterprise in its use. This course was based
on two implicit assumptions. The first was that any
piece of God's outdoors not actual swamp or desert
would reward the expenditure of agricultural labor and
capital. The second assumption was that there was a
potential if not imminent scarcity of land. With the
advancing technique of scientific and mechanized agriculture and advancing knowledge of farm organization and management we are coming to realize that
we can get the maximum economic product with the

minimum of effort and cost by applying agricultural labor and capital to certain more limited areas carefully selected with reference to their technological character and market location.

During the agricultural depression millions of acres of land have reverted to government—county, State, or national—through the inability of former owners to pay taxes or perfect homestead entries. In this moment of retreat from exploited colonization areas there must come some perception of the futility of attempting to wring an adequate living from any and all lands by the process of farming. Practically all the reverted acres, however, have gone into what the stock market would call "weak hands." The government officials of a State with a large submarginal area cannot possibly be counted upon to hold such lands a moment beyond the time when the first sign of reviving agricultural prices tempts unwary settlers to stake their fortunes on a cheap farm. Still more will county officials be eager to get a few dollars per acre in sales price or the payment of arrears of taxes and the prospect of taxpayers for a few years ahead. Furthermore, there is an enormous area of land no less submarginal which will remain in the hands of private holders throughout the depression period but be thrown open to exploitative development at the earliest opportunity for sale.

What manufacturer could face the future if his factory stood in the midst of idle plants which could be thrown back into production in competition with him upon such cutthroat terms the moment prices got back toward a remunerative basis? Unless we can devise such land policies as will give the body of suitably located and adequately equipped farmers reasonable protection against speculative operations below the margin, the business of agriculture will remain in a demoralized condition for many years in the future.

Congress has been asked to repeal the Homestead law as a first step toward remedying this situation. Such action, however, would be hardly more than a gesture. To be effective it would need to be followed by an extensive program for enlargement of the public domain by acquisition of all those submarginal lands not under the control of states or minor units of government. In only a few instances is any agency less than the Federal government adequate to cope with the problem. New York State has already acquired several million acres and, within a reasonable time in the future, could and let us hope will go on to double or treble this area and thus deal effectively with the problem. This, however, is done by a very rich state with an enormous city population eager to use public parks and playgrounds. The situation is harder in the three Lake states with their vast cut-over areas. It is staggering in a poor state like Arkansas, with a thin population, low per capita wealth, and a big area of waste land. It is impossible in terms of anything other than Federal acquisition in Nevada, where 51 million acres, or 72 per cent of the total area of the state, is even now in public hands. The enormous importance of this problem of control of the margin of land use is matched by the gigantic figures involved. To retrace our steps from the free land régime of the past to a situation of social control in the future would involve the acquisition of some 250 million acres and its proper maintenance and administration permanently.

The attainment of such a goal must be remote indeed. Meanwhile, we may derive at least a little satisfaction from the fact that national thinking is turning in this direction. A national conference on land utilization was held last autumn at the call of the Secretary of Agriculture, and it has led to the appointment of two standing committees—a Land Use Planning Committee and an Advisory and Legislative Committee on Land Use.

What we have been saying thus far relates to the farmer's position as proprietor and operator. There is, however, another major division of our agricultural platform, and this concerns his position with reference to markets and prices. This problem may be considered from two points of view—one domestic and the other foreign. The former focuses sharply on coöperative marketing organizations and the Farm Board; the other on international market influences—reparations, international debts, and the tariff.

As for coöperation, it should be looked upon as a bulwark of strength in the agricultural organization of the future, bringing to the farmer and his inherently small-scale business enterprise the major advantages of large-scale business which industry and trade have developed through the corporation. Unfortunately, coöperation has been badly misrepresented and oversold to our farmers as a quick and easy form of economic magic. They have been led to expect the impossible in the way of price maintenance and encouraged to think that they could get the benefits of coöperation by signing on the dotted line rather than joining themselves in participating groups to hammer out certain very workaday business betterments. It was but natural that

62

legislators and political and farm-organization leaders should have turned with relief to coöperation as the "sure cure" for agricultural distress. It is unfortunate, however, that the Farm Board, which was intrusted with the generalship of this great movement, should have known so little of the true nature of coöperation. In its eagerness to make speed it tried to start the car in high. The inevitable result followed. Progress—if any—has been disappointingly slow, while serious, if not irreparable, injury has been done to the mechanism. Widespread coöperative organization in agriculture should still be kept as a major plank in our agricultural program, but effort should be turned toward broad education and the affording of helpful facilities equally to all voluntary groups. There should be an end of high-pressure promotion of certain favored undertakings under bureaucratic direction.

As to foreign influences impinging on the farmer's market and agricultural prices, the difficulty is acute. The farmer's interest demands such freeing of world-wide commerce and industry as will restore purchasing power for his products. Reparations and interallied debts are the crux of the problem. We must abandon unreasonable insistence upon literal fulfillment of a bond whose terms were dictated by political considerations and war psychology. Economically they are impossible to carry out, and the continued insistence upon them simply postpones the day of general business recovery. *Wallaces' Farmer* recently stated the farmer's true interest in this matter editorially with clarity and force. Mr. Wallace said:

"I would like to see us get some good out of the debts which England and France owe us, but unless the United States is willing to reduce very greatly her tariff and also cut down on her exports of wheat, lard, cotton, and manufactured products, I am quite certain that these debts will never be paid. Also, I am quite certain that the big income taxpayers themselves would be decidedly ahead of the game to pay $250,000,000 a year extra income taxes, because of the fact that the international confidence which would follow on a more definite settling of the war debt and the German reparations would make such good business that the profits of our big corporations would be increased by many times the $250,000,000 extra income tax."

And elsewhere:

"We urge Congress to use these debts owed to the United States government by the European nations to help instead of to harm us, as has been the case during recent years. Low prices this winter are probably due more than anything else to the ignorant way in which Congress has handled the war-debt situation."

If we are to effect the transition from the rôle of debtor to that of creditor nation gracefully and well, we shall have to break up many old habits of thought and patterns of action. Agriculture did well in the emergency years just after the war to get some tariff protection to cushion the shock of its drastic readjustment. Further gains from the same device are out of the question. The farmer's immediate tariff interest lies in the lowering of industrial duties. But from now on it should be insisted that any tariff, industrial or agricultural, is to be defended only on the basis of special circumstances touching the position of that commodity and its producing group in the light of national policy. No longer can we start from the assumption of protected industry and free-trade agriculture.

The world outlook as to agricultural production promises that supplies will be heavy and the price trend weak for some years in the future. As we said at the outset, agriculture cannot "raise itself by its own bootstraps" and drag the rest of the economic system up to prosperity. Its own prosperity must wait the day when the industrial world puts itself back to work. But if reasonable intelligence is applied toward reviving employment both at home and abroad and unclogging international commerce, and toward guiding geographical readjustment and equalizing fixed charges at home, through some or all of the measures which we have been discussing, farmers will again stand the chance of establishing an adequate income basis for a standard of living approximating that of which they had a taste for a few years prior to 1920, and not grossly inferior to that of the town.

WALTON H. HAMILTON

is professor of law at Yale University. He was professor of economics at Amherst College from 1915 to 1923, and at the Robert Brookings Graduate School of Economics and Government from 1923 to 1928. He is the author of "Current Economic Problems," *and coauthor with H. R. Wright of* "A Way of Order for Bituminous Coal."

Big Business and the Anti-Trust Laws

A FEW months ago the staid United States Supreme Court took "judicial notice" of the depression. It found "the change in conditions" to be "the outstanding fact, dominating thought and action throughout the country." A little later, in a dissenting opinion, Mr. Justice Brandeis declared that "the people of the United States are confronted with an emergency more serious than war." He did not attempt to catalogue reasons for our current plight or to impute blame; but he did set it down that, "rightly or wrongly, many persons insist that one of the major contributing causes has been unbridled competition." And he did assert that "there must be power in the States and the nation" to correct "the evils of excess productive capacity" and "through experimentation" to "remold our economic practices and institutions to meet changing social needs." In this restrained expression of judicial opinion a sense and reason which is current challenges a sense and reason which is outworn.

Out anti-trust laws express the common sense of another age. Toward the close of the nineteenth century a nation which had been composed of farmers and small business men was confronted by a crisis. A revolution

66

in the ways of production which had been gaining momentum with the passing decades was no longer to be ignored. The hand trades were giving way to manufacture; the machine process was transforming the ways of production; businesses were becoming great corporations; captains of industry were coming into possession of wealth and power; and the strange and wicked city was dominating the country. A society made up of almost self-sufficient farms, with its complement of local trade, was being transformed into an articulate, even if rather unruly, industrial system. In the whirl of change small traders who saw their enterprises crowded to the wall cried out against the iniquities of big business. The public, which distrusted size as much as it feared extortionate price, realized that untoward things were going forward. An industrialism, which had got its start by stealth, came on with such a rush as to leave the people bewildered. The world was no longer as it used to be—and ought to be—and it was high time that something was done about it.

In the emergency a policy had to be formulated. In the task it seemed to occur to no one, at least among those in strategic places, to ask whether industrialism was not rather different from anything society had known before, and whether experimentation might not be used to contrive for it a suitable scheme of control. Instead, the thinkers and the statesmen of the times brought to the problem the best wisdom they could muster—and this wisdom was the product of a social experience which was passing. If the farmer found difficulty in making ends meet, or the small merchant was

67

threatened with extinction, or the customer had his pocket picked by the extortionate dealer, or the working-man put in his long hours for a pittance, it was all because the system of free competition was not working. The trusts, or Wall Street, or "the hydra-headed monster monopoly" was the villain in the piece. The people had only to banish "the hydra-headed monster," and the natural laws of supply and demand could be depended upon to make industries orderly instruments of national well-being.

At the time, the case for an enforced competition seemed to be quite reasonable. Fact may be on time, but thought usually arrives on the scene a little late. The people talked quite grandly about every man being "the architect of his fate"; and they believed quite sincerely in the creed of "each for himself and the devil take the hindmost." In that climate of opinion only individualistic notions of the province of government and the control of industry could gain currency. Moreover, a long experience with petty trade had produced its own economic policy, and the sense of the man in the street was confirmed by the wisdom in the learned books. It was perfectly clear that the competition of seller with seller and of buyer with buyer gave assurance of efficient service, high quality, and fair price. The interests of one party to a trade—seller, lender, or employer—were balanced by the interests of the other party—buyer, borrower, or employee. Nor could any trader help himself at the expense of his customer, for his desire for gain was checked by the rivalry of others for the very dollars he was trying to secure. The ups and downs in prices which came in the wake of competition attracted

68

or repelled capital, and thus in each industry kept the capacity-to-produce adjusted to the demand for the product. In fact, free enterprise was "a great and beneficent system" which kept industries organized, eliminated the inefficient, gave survival to the fit, insured to labor good working conditions and fair wages, and protected the consumer. For all "the blessings of free competition," as the Supreme Court of the nineties called them, a single provision had to be made. Trades were to be kept open, if need be through a legally enforced competition, and an automatic, self-regulating system could be depended upon to secure for the public all the business system had to give. The thing to be done seemed obvious; and an attempt was made to stay the development of large-scale enterprise and to make big business behave as if it were petty trade.

So it was that in the name of laissez faire the law was invoked. For some time, even if not from time immemorial, the common law had forbidden "conspiracies in restraint of trade," and a number of States had in the decades following the Civil War aimed statutes at the growing evil of monopoly. In 1890 the Sherman Act, designed to prohibit combinations in "commerce among the several States," was enacted into law. In 1914 the Clayton and the Federal Trade Commission acts were passed in an attempt to extend and to strengthen the federal anti-trust act. The great majority of the States—almost all in the South and West—passed their little Sherman acts. On grand or miniature scale the prohibition of trusts, combinations, and monopoly became a part of the law of the land.

The resort to law carried its own peculiar hazards.

69

The ideas of common sense had to be translated into the language of legislation; the ends of public policy had to be vindicated through a process of litigation. Economists and statesmen might talk of an enforced competition, but the judiciary gave its attention to "conspiracies" in "restraint of trade." The language of the statutes caused the courts to consider modern industrial mergers in the light of precedents from a pre-industrial era. The holdings of a former age were invoked in suits to punish offenders or to "dissolve" monopolies; the proof had to be by rules of evidence which had been contrived to get at the truth in matters of a quite different kind; the litigation had to go forward, from issue to issue and from court to court, under a formal code of procedure never designed to draw a line between desirable and undesirable forms of industrial organizations. The cases were heard before benches of judges far more experienced in the discipline of the law than in business, and far better acquainted with Cooley on Blackstone than with texts on the economics of monopoly. It is hardly strange that questions of anti-social practices were subordinated to the antecedent questions of decorous procedure, and that ingenious attorneys found ways to "wear the case out" before the larger issues were ever raised. The course of justice is unhurried; its judgments condemn only specific practices. A business enterprise, blessed with able counsel, may nimbly employ alternative devices as yet free from legal disapproval to achieve its acquisitive ends.

It is small wonder that the resort to law has not been a conspicuous success. Our era of federal "trust-busting" covers a period of more than forty years. In this period

has occurred the greatest movement in the concentration
of productive wealth known to history. Yet the statistics
of the Department of Justice present a most illuminating picture of law enforcement at work. A little more
than ten score criminals have been jailed, and eight have
fallen afoul of the law for contempt—a matter of a little
more than one person a year. A little under 1,400 persons have had to pay fines aggregating about $1,570,000
—or roughly 40 offenders and $50,000 a year. A ship-
ment of 175 cases of cigarettes was confiscated under the
terms of the Sherman Act, but later released under
bond. A number of States have derived far more revenue
from trust-busting than has the federal government.
Yet the prosecution of cases has not been a profit-mak-
ing enterprise; the fines collected have fallen far short
of the costs of administration. Current receipts are only
a pittance of what the traffic in "conspiracies in restraint
of trade" might be made to bear; yet the Secretary of
the Treasury, anxious to balance his budget, can hardly
look upon it hopefully as a source of revenue. On its
face this record is a glorious tribute of respect paid by
men of big business to the letter, if not to the spirit,
of the anti-trust acts.

This does not mean that the statutes have been without their effect upon the practices of business. They have
been ineffectual in preventing corporations from ac-
quiring the physical properties of their competitors and
in staying the progress of industrial combination. They
have put serious obstacles in the way of agreement
among rival manufacturers to restrict output and to
maintain price. The barriers have not been insuperable;
captains of industry are anxious to live within the law,

but they also love to have their own way, and the art of doing both is not unknown to able lawyers. If resourcefulness has often failed the emergency, the credit is not always due to the law. The ups and downs of business strain the morale of all industrial groups; and lapses into the established ways of competition are due more often to a break in discipline from within than to the vigilance of public officials. It is of interest that a number of gigantic corporations have escaped the toils of the law, and that severe penalties have often fallen upon small businesses and upon trade unions. Even where they have not been effective the acts have been at least a petty nuisance to the interests affected.

But the roots of failure are far more fundamental than a resort to law to give effect to a public policy. The course of industrialism has come with too much of a rush to be stayed; its forces have been too turbulent to be subdued by legislative fiat and court decree; business men have been too powerful to allow their activities to be crowded into the grooves chiseled out long ago for a simpler industry. The universe of petty trade was one sort of place; the world of big business is quite another. In the small town the trader knew his customers personally; he could enlarge his business as his market expanded; his out-of-pocket expenses furnished adequate bases for his prices. As invention brought changes in technical processes, time allowed an easy accommodation. Under the prevailing system a knowledge of the future intent of customers and of the hidden plans of rivals are essential to a sound policy. The business judgments of today determine the capacity-to-produce of tomorrow; yet, in an impersonal market, the demand may go to a rival or pass on to another ware. In many lines of business overhead costs have become dominant; and as fixed charges are spread over a large or a small output, the market determines the unit cost of production, rather than the unit cost the market. In adapting the capacity-to-produce of an industry to the demand for goods, a far neater and less wasteful adjustment is demanded than the separate judgments of business rivals can effect. They must respond just enough, and not too much, to market trends, and the unity in action essential to order cannot be secured by a policy of competition.

In fact, the competitive system at work presents problems unknown to the competitive system in books. The good people of the nineties were disturbed because rivals might get together and conspire to impose extortionate prices upon their customers; and that danger still exists. But quite as important is the bill of costs which competition imposes upon the producers. It makes for plant waste and surplus capacity; it fails to articulate tidy establishments into orderly industries. A capacity which cries to be used and overhead costs which click on with the clock lead as often as not to an overdone competition which drives prices relentlessly down. In its wake comes a plague of bankruptcies, irregular employment, and wages too low to support a decent standard of life. Under such conditions there is no chance to get answered, or even to have raised, the larger questions of policy which affect all who have a stake in the industry. It makes all who are concerned—executives, salaried officials, investors, laborers, and consumers—creatures of an undirected industrialism.

73

The cry today is for a revision of the statutes; and yet that revision is no easy matter. An influential group demands that trade agreements be submitted to an official body, such as the Federal Trade Commission, and that advance opinions be given upon the legality of the proposed practices. The proposal has much to recommend it; the bother is that it will probably fail in operation. The spokesman for the government is likely to be guided in his advice by what the courts have said in the past, and to hand down general and platitudinous statements which have little relation to the novel practices for which approval is sought. A business must meet changing conditions; its policies must be adapted to the course of events as they emerge; a declaration that a policy on paper is legal can hardly apply to the policy as it works out in practice. Another group demands the right to "exchange information" and promises to abstain from a regulation of output and a control of price. The bother is that, if discipline can be sustained and resourceful lawyers can be retained, the practice prayed for is all that is needed to effect a rather far-reaching monopoly. A third group boldly demands the repeal of the acts and offers no constructive scheme with which to replace them. It insists upon enlarging the control of business over industry when recent events have proved the incapacity of business for the proper exercise of the control it already possesses. The anti-trust statutes are a declaration that business is affected with a public interest; the moral commitment of that declaration is much too important to be lost.

But no mere expedients can get to the heart of the problem. The demand for change comes from an industrial world; it is not to be met with the devices and procedures of a craft society. The simple idea of the uniformity of all trades, which underlies current legislation, must give way to an accommodation of public control to the varying necessities of different industries. For our businesses are not all alike; banking, railroads, power, and radio-broadcasting have already been accorded their own schemes of control. The methods of production and of marketing in various other trades— building, retailing, milk, coal, textiles, cotton-planting —have their own peculiarities, with which the problem of industrial direction must come to grips. In all cases, if there is to be order, if the nuisance of bankruptcy is to be abated, if workingmen are to have regular jobs and adequate wages, there must be some central direction. The formal control, or understanding, must certainly extend to capacity, probably to output, and possibly to price. In all cases, if there is to be flexibility, there must be some control. It is essential that in all matters relating primarily to the establishment, discretion shall be close to the facts.

This general end is to be served by no simple and uniform economic organization. We have ceased to think in terms of panaceas; and neither a return to the good old competitive system of our fathers or the adoption of a ready-made, hand-me-down substitute will meet current need. If our industries are to become instruments of national well-being, we must employ a varied program of economic control. Three distinct types of organization seem to be promising. Industries which produce non-essentials and can win only a limited trade against the allurements of unlike wares demand little

75

public control; their activities may well be intrusted to the capricious solicitude of the market. Industries, such as railroads and power, which are linked with all the activities of the economic order demand a large social oversight; this may be met either by an administration commission or by public ownership. Industries, such as coal and steel, which have distinctive groups of customers may be organized from within under a control in which producers and consumers alike share. Industries must be kept going and their dependents must be given adequate livings; consumers must be accorded protection against an anti-social restriction of output and a monopoly element in price. This problem is not to be solved by any "either this or that" formula; its solution demands clear vision, full knowledge, and neat adjustments. Above all it demands the capacities of men skilled in social invention.

The plain truth of the matter is that the rewriting of the anti-trust laws is the beginning, not the end, of the problem. We may indulge in tinkering and console ourselves with make-believe and pretense; but the fundamental question stands out in clear-cut relief. Today a lack of harmony exists between the technology of industry and its organization. An economic order in which the productive processes belong to big business and the arrangements for its control to petty trade cannot abide. We cannot banish depression and summon order by invoking the ideas which the people of the 1890's borrowed from a small town culture. We must devise a scheme adequate to the task of the direction of great industry. In a world of change a society cannot live upon a wisdom borrowed from our fathers.

H. PARKER WILLIS

is professor of banking at Columbia University. He was formerly editor-in-chief of the New York Journal of Commerce, and served as expert for the House Banking and Currency Committee in the drafting of the Federal Reserve Act; later becoming Secretary of the Federal Reserve Board 1914-1928, and Economist 1918-1922.

What Shall We Do with Our Banks?

To THE man who is willing to read financial history "with his eyes and not with his prejudices," it is increasingly evident that the banking question in the United States has reached a turning of the road. For a good while past, the pathway has dipped steadily downward. Our banking system has grown less manageable and less efficient, less solvent, less reliable either as a keeper of money or as a user of it. Our Federal Reserve banks have shown less and less leadership, and have grown more and more dependent upon the wishes and inclinations, expressed or implied, of small cliques drawn from the financial interests of the larger cities. The result has been an individualism exaggerated at times into something approaching chaos. It is foolish to speak of this result as "inevitable" or "irresistible." No other country—not even Austria—has had any such experience as ours, though many have suffered from false financial policies of every sort. We, with the greatest gold stock in the world's history, and with the most wealth and a very low average per capita debt, have suffered most from failures, incompetence, inability to regulate either our domestic or our international relationships in banking and money.

7

The forward path in our banking development now forks sharply. One branch leads further downward to complete disorganization. The other climbs steeply to a level of greater wholesomeness and safety. It will not be easy to pursue this latter. Yet we must follow the more difficult road unless we are willing to let our whole economic order be further disorganized and disturbed. Professor Marshall has said that money and banking are the nucleus around which all economic science clusters. He would also say, we may be sure, that practical, sound management of money and banking is the nucleus around which all successful economic policy intended for the betterment of the community, or even for its protection in present well-being, must cluster, and on which it directly depends. What, then, are the elements of a sound and safe banking development for the welfare of the United States in the early coming years? What must we seek to do during the next four or five years as a practical task?

It has already been seen and admitted by forward-looking men that the first and great commandment of banking soundness in this country will be the ending of the century-long conflict on banking oversight between the States and the central government. Some one self-consistent policy must control; and it requires no sage to see that this policy will be most easily attained through the transfer of power over banking legislation to the federal government. Lacking such a formal transfer, there must be found some means of agreement between the State legislatures and the federal authority whereby there will be uniformity of action and over-

78

sight, and whereby all banks will be affiliated with our federal system on terms helpful to them. Without this step we shall go on with the conflict between grades of government, with the attempt on the part of the States to tempt banks away from their federal charters, with the effort of national administrators to draw them back by laxity in law or in administration, with the craven fear on the part of the Federal Reserve System lest it lose members through uprightness of administration, and with other elements of profound weakness that must ultimately bring disorganization even more complete than that now existing. We might attain the desired unity by a constitutional amendment that would vest all power over banking in the federal government—this then to be followed by complete revision of present banking enactments—or we might get a similar outcome through some movement headed by a wise and strong President in some future Administration that would bring about identity of organization, and identity of action on a code of uniform banking legislation.

To hope and work for some such result is certainly not utopian nor even unpractical, yet it is clear that by hitching our banking-reform wagon to such a star we shall accomplish our ends but slowly. It is hard, in the first place, to educate those who are but moderately interested in banking to the point where they are willing to see the need of any such procedure. It is still more difficult to induce public men to commit themselves to actual steps in behalf of any such far-off divine event. The desired result may be attained, but it probably will be only after much more sad experience and bank misery, unless there shall come some sudden and unexpected illumination of the problem that will convince even the wayfaring man, though a fool, that a major operation would be the shortest way to the relief of what is one of the chief underlying difficulties of contemporary American economic civilization. Moreover, suppose it were possible to get the desired constitutional amendment tomorrow, what should be done under it—what changes should we make?

We shall not be too opportunistic, therefore, if, while awaiting some working out along this indicated line— and, it may be added, some change of feeling in Congress that would permit wise legislation after such a constitutional change as that indicated had been effected —we formulate to ourselves some more immediately resultful program as a basis of practical procedure. Suppose, then, we assume, as so many insist upon assuming, that we shall always have to struggle with a condition in which there is a dual control of banking, with forty-nine competing jurisdictions seeking to "attract" banks to their "systems" by laxity in law or administration.

If, accordingly, we determine to work along this narrow line, it seems necessary, first of all, to bring about a direct and positive supervision and regulation of banking that will relieve the community from the terrible suffering and danger that has been, and is daily, inflicted upon it by banking mismanagement and failure. Within the past year we have had some 2,300 closings of banks, and we have enlisted in an army of discontent, it is estimated, approximately 6,000,000 persons who were depositors in the banks closed since the beginning of the panic and who are now deprived of the use of their funds. It seems obvious that the adoption of means to correct this crying evil must be resorted to. Frank thought, free of the evasions of selfish economic metaphysics, brings us inevitably to one of two conclusions: (1) since the unprofessional depositor has not the means to judge accurately the soundness of his bank, and since wholesale bank failure is disastrous to both economic and social order, some means of stopping bank failures must be found in governmental provisions that will either guarantee depositors against loss or at least provide them with immediate means of getting the worth of their claims as soon as a bank is closed; (2) there must be such a reorganization of the banking system as to insure—humanly speaking—that failures shall be rare episodes.

There is good reason for rejecting the notion of "bank-deposit guaranty." Not only is it repugnant to those who believe in the soundness and effectiveness of individual choice of banks as possibly the best means of indirectly keeping them in order (despite the lack of criteria of judgment already mentioned), but the experience with the plan that has now been quite extensively had among the States has shown it to be, generally speaking, unsuccessful. The federal government might do better with such a guaranty or it might not. In any case, the presumption is against the project. In lieu of such a resort to extremes, we have the alternative of establishing a banking régime not subject to failures or of applying severe and stringent legislative regulation to the business of banking, of such a nature that there will be an entirely different type of management. What the general nature of this regulation should

81

be we shall presently suggest. The other proposal—that of so reorganizing our banking as to produce a system that is failure-proof—is in some ways more attractive. It has been found entirely possible in such countries as Canada and Great Britain largely to eliminate bank failures, and to lay upon the banks as a body the duty of absorbing those of their number which are on the verge of failure, so as to save the community from suffering. To do that in the United States is nearly out of the question, for the reason that it would imply the very great centralization of our banking system. There are today far too many banks in this country for strength or safety, and they are, in a vast majority of cases, much too weak, with over-small capital and scanty resources. They are not large enough to resist the strain of depression in many cases, even if they have been fairly well managed in times of industrial and economic peace. It seems, however, almost certain that the people of the United States will not self-consciously endure the risk, as they conceive it, of great centralization in banking, even if assured that thereby they may escape a considerable share of the dangers of failure. Branch banking is a way of bringing about concentration and should be tried as fast as the public will permit. This drives us back to the application of satisfactory regulation as the most immediate measure of reform, even though a good deal can and should be done by making access to the banking profession far more difficult for incompetents and exploiters than now.

Given, however, a specified banking structure, the tendency to failure already spoken of is in part the outgrowth and in part the accompaniment or effect of a

82

national vice—the disposition to speculate. Bankers of all classes have found it easier to "make money"—as they thought—by dabbling in the securities markets than by following the slow, painful course of financing business and discounting commercial paper. They have of late years (1) invested too heavily in stock-exchange securities, and (2) over-heavily financed those who were speculating beyond their means in these same issues—and in others. Inasmuch as we have as yet no means of controlling or limiting or regulating the issue of securities, and inasmuch as over-issue will, under existing conditions, probably always continue as a perennial evil of stock-market finance, it is clear that the banks which hold the public's money must in some wise be divorced from stock-market operations. To accomplish such a result apparently means that they must be separated into two groups—one which does not accept deposits but is allowed to finance industry, and a second which accepts deposits and carries on commercial banking but does not engage in market operations or in financing those who do. Moreover, since a study of failures shows that among the primary causes of such failures are found, directly or indirectly, the market operations of banks, we are led once more to the conclusion that the immediate or expedient way of starting the reform of banking for the purpose of prompt relief is through the control of the technique of actual bank operation of which we have spoken above—and a discussion of which was then promised.

What ought this type of control to be? There need be no hesitation in answering such a question. First of all, there is more and more ground for feeling that

83

banking is too hazardous a profession to be left open to any ignoramus or favorite son—or son-in-law—who knows nothing about it. The "Wisconsin idea" of licensing bankers has been ridiculed but has much to commend it. If we license plumbers, engineers, public accountants, lawyers, and doctors, why should we not throw around the banking profession some safeguards of personnel? There is ample reason for so doing.

With qualified men at the head, there is still a need for meticulous regulation of our deposit banks. They ought not to be allowed to apply the depositors' funds in any way that will bring them into unreasonable hazard. There is every reason, therefore, for careful specification and regulation of the types and classes of securities they may buy. The desirable thing will be, as soon as practical, to make our deposit banks entirely free of the business of receiving and caring for savings, and to let them serve only the demand-deposit needs of the community. In such a case, the field of their investments will be narrow, for they will then be bound to deal almost wholly in commercial paper and in very short term obligations of carefully specified nature. To make their efforts safer even in that restricted field we should generalize or universalize our false-statement laws and require by law what is now the custom among American banks—the interchange of credit information. We should compel the filing of truthful statements by applicants for loans and in every way we should endeavor to protect banking operations.

It may take a good while to separate deposit banking from investment banking, demand deposits from savings, but there should at least be no serious trouble

84

in introducing departmentalized banking somewhat after the California plan. If, however, even this involves too much social effort, and if we insist on permitting banks to continue to receive savings or time deposits along with demand, pending the more complete change of general policy already indicated, their purchases of securities must follow the already well-developed requirements of savings-bank operations, and the savings or time depositor should be given a first lien on the assets which represent his funds, that he may have all possible safety in case of failure.

It seems hardly needful to add that in such a situation as is thus described the banker should in no circumstances be permitted to engage in any "back-door" or "back-stairs" banking. He should not, in other words, be suffered to have an interest in an affiliated concern which may do all those things that are forbidden to him, and to which he freely lends the funds for the carrying on of all those activities in which he himself is technically not permitted to engage. "Affiliates" must be separated from their "parent" banks and discouraged entirely, whenever and wherever possible under our dual State and federal jurisdiction. The least that can be done for the moment is to end the system of joint ownership or control and to insist that an affiliate shall borrow from a bank only on the same terms and to the same extent as others. It is deeply regrettable that banking opinion has not already thus discouraged them, or made them impossible. Perhaps it may yet do so, as is suggested by some recent cases in which affiliated concerns have been given up, especially in New York City. But while waiting for such a growth of opinion, the law ought not to hesitate. Stock-market operations, underwriting of securities, dabbling in all kinds of undesirable or dangerous schemes must be abandoned by our bankers, whether they act in the bank itself or in some related enterprise.

Above all else, there is needed much more careful protection of the present trust-company operations, in such a way as to insure the safeguarding of the funds of deceased persons or of persons with trust funds to their credit who require the service of a trustee. Present conditions are exceedingly unfavorable to such persons. It is true, as asserted in much of the trust-company advertising of the present day, that a trust company never dies or disappears as may an individual executor or trustee. It may, however, be added that the individual never merges or changes his whole type of being. The trust company does, and it has often happened of late years that a man placed his property in trust and sailed away or retired serene in the confidence that his property was in the hands of conservative men, only to find within a short time the company sold out and combined with another where the men in charge were of a different type and where funds were likely to be used for totally new purposes whenever choice was discretionary. The practice of making securities in one affiliate of an enterprise and buying them for trust account—directly or indirectly—in another, is too common, and must be ended.

We have already noted that, with the changes that have been above suggested, the business of dealing in securities ought to be relegated to another group of institutions. This suggests the desirability of an entirely new type of banking house whose mission it should be to finance long-term obligations, carry on foreign-trade finance, issue securities for purchase by investors willing to take some risks, and generally to finance and serve the capital market. For this purpose adequate, moderate federal legislation is desirable. It should be uniform for the whole country, and should aim chiefly (1) to protect the investor from false representations; (2) to prevent the deposit bank from becoming involved in securities operations; and (3) to prohibit unfair company regulations, control by small cliques through unfair voting arrangements, and the like. It is evident that all companies doing an interstate trade should be required to keep their books on a uniform prescribed plan, somewhat as do the railroads, and to make full and complete statements to stockholders. Financing in open market should be contingent upon compliance with reasonable requirements of this sort.

Nothing has thus far been said herein of the question of our Federal Reserve banks and their management. The subject has of late been widely and technically discussed. This is no place for the continuation of a purely technical analysis of that important phase of our banking problem. Those who want to pursue the inquiry thoroughly and with evidence for each step toward a conclusion will find in Part VI of the Hearings before the Senate Banking and Currency Subcommittee of 1931-32 the full statement of the current policy of Federal Reserve banks as set forth in their own words. Suffice it to say, for the purposes of this article, that the reserve banks have wandered far from their original purpose, and have become primarily stock-market auxiliaries, discounting but sparingly for their city and larger member institutions, and scarcely at all for country institutions, while the latter get less and less benefit from the system. Their main activities, particularly in the larger cities, and conspicuously in New York City, are those of helping the stock and money markets by letting out funds or adjusting rates, as opportunity seems to require or permit. Their influence, of which great things were once hoped, in preventing or warding off bank failures, has proven wholly illusory.

This is a situation that gravely impairs the efficiency of our banking system and threatens its solidity and safety for the future. It is also at odds with the conception of a restored soundness on the part of the smaller institutions which, as already explained, are likely to continue as an outstanding feature of the American banking scene for a good while. Probably the fundamental error was made originally when reserve banks were permitted to abstain from dealing with the public, and when they were forbidden the supervision of private stockholders. Their shares ought unquestionably to be thrown open to private subscription, and they should at the same time be compelled to engage in direct dealings with the public. Thereby the business men and the smaller bankers would be encouraged to offer them the right kind of paper, and thus to attract their funds directly into business, instead of putting them through the stock-market strainer and perhaps spoiling that strainer in the process. In default of some such far-reaching reform as this—which, after all, would merely introduce here something like the system that has lasted more than a century and a quarter in France and far

88

longer in Great Britain, with success—it should at least be possible to revise the system in such a way as to insure a commercial-banking preference on the part of the reserve banks, a greater degree of independence on the part of the smaller and more remote reserve institutions, and a better and more professional management on behalf of all.

If we now retrace our steps and sum up the chief points in the program thus set forth we shall see that it shapes up somewhat as follows (although here presented in an order different from that employed in the preceding discussion):

1. Revise the Federal Reserve Act so as to insure more direct dealings with the commercial banks; and if possible with the actual borrowers of the country.

a. Let this be done by restricting the channels of market operation, and broadening those of commercial operation.

b. Let it be accompanied by a reorganization of personnel such as to insure greater ability in charge of the reserve banks and better professional quality in the personnel of all banks.

2. As soon as feasible, secure a constitutional amendment that will permit Congressional legislation on banking for the whole country. When this is attained, compel all banks to affiliate themselves with the Federal Reserve System, in one capacity or another.

3. Pending the attainment of such an amendment, lose no time in developing a system of adequate investment-banking regulation that will apply to our commercial banks, members of the Reserve System, the

same kind and quality, at least, of restriction in their investment-banking activities that has already been applied to their commercial-paper operations.

4. The chief feature of this regulation should be action designed to render it difficult or impossible for them to continue in the development of stock-market affiliations and operations, and to oblige them to confine their activities to commercial-paper and very short-term transactions practically exclusively.

5. Non-deposit banking with permission to issue and underwrite securities, to sell and deal in bonds and other evidences of long-term debt should then be encouraged as an independent type of organization under federal uniform supervision. Corporate bookkeeping on a uniform basis and truthful public statements of condition should be an essential.

6. "Affiliates" or allied enterprises should by no means be permitted to continue to operate in connection with their "parent" commercial banks.

7. Appropriate improvement of bank examination and supervision, State and national, with additional administrative safeguards, should be at once and thoroughly applied, the object being to prevent bank failures of the wholesale sort from which the community now suffers.

8. Incidentally, let there be provided a suitable organization for purchasing and liquidating bank assets without subjecting the public to the losses and inconveniences inherent in present methods.

This program is moderate. It calls only for the minimum measures of reorganization demanded by existing conditions. Every one of the changes provided is required in the interest of restoration of prosperity. There is nothing extreme, nothing "radical" in any of the notions thus expressed. They are all in line with sound and conservative banking principle—all indorsed at one time or another by most cautious men. They ought to be absolutely demanded and put into effect as the result of the coming Presidential campaign. The only thing new or striking about them would be their incorporation as a general program—interrelated and calculated to be effective.

We have left until the last the problem of the monetary policy of the United States. It is a large problem and one on which it will be well to avoid dogmatism. Nevertheless, a few major points are certain. We must continue on the gold standard until an unquestionably superior and effective plan shall have made its appearance. If, meanwhile, there should prove to be a possibility of restoring the gold standard throughout the Western world, we should join actively in making it workable. This need not in any way prejudice our deciding to give up the gold standard in the future should we hit upon an admittedly superior substitute. It would merely remedy intolerable conditions pending a general decision to change policy. If, while awaiting the time for the development of such a substitute, the recession of prices and the suffering thereby caused becomes intolerable, let us remedy it by breaking down excessive prices which are the result of combination and agreement—or failing in that, let us get a change of price level if it *must be* (which the present writer does not admit) by changing the gold content of our unit of value, rather than by inflating our banking system and tinkering with prices behind the scenes to the great profits of special groups.

All this may be properly deferred until we have accomplished the duty nearest to our hand—the reorganization of our banking system in the interests of safety, fairness, and equitable treatment of the depositor, investor, and saver. It would not help these groups to provide a "managed currency" or any other substitute for our present standard of value, if our banking should remain, as now, disorganized, unsafe, and selfish.

MORRIS LLEWELLYN COOKE

is a Philadelphia consulting engineer. He was director of the Giant Power Survey in Pennsylvania; and is now a Trustee of the Power Authority of the State of New York.

Planning for Power

THE COLLAPSE of the valuation and holding-company rackets and the emergence of the small consumer as the arbiter of power policy are the high points in the current utility situation. Transportation rates are less and less affected either by the cost or by the present value of property used and useful in rendering the service, while the electric, gas, and telephone industries consider unfair the basing of rates on the reproduction-cost basis which until the 1929 debacle was touted as the equitable "law of the land." Most of the important arguments heretofore advanced in favor of the holding companies have been exploded, and these companies are at grips with seemingly insuperable difficulties.

If electric rates, at present highly discriminatory against the small user, can be regulated so as to approach the standard of cost plus a fair profit, consumption can be so increased as not only to eliminate the drudgery of housework but to pave the way for a new artistry in living for even modest homes. Through low-priced current for the farms agriculture can be energized and the cultural level of our rural population radically improved. In this atmosphere of change, planning offers great possibilities for a public conscious of its power.

Special interest attaches to public planning for the utilities because their activities can now legally be reg-

93

ulated by public authority. In this field many of the constitutional prohibitions against interference by public authority with private business do not hold. The most important appeals from commission and court findings in utility cases have been based on claims of confiscation sought to be resisted under the Fourteenth, or "due process," Amendment to the Constitution. Only those private undertakings invested—or as one typesetter put it "infested"—with a public interest may be regulated by public authority. The United States Supreme Court recently decided by a six to two vote that the State of Oklahoma could not regulate ice companies. The dissenting opinion of Justice Brandeis, concurred in by Justice Stone, will long continue to constitute an illuminating text favorable to widening the areas of State experimentation in the public control of quasi-private company practices.

Possibly as much as one-fifth of the productive and transportation capacity of the country is now included in the utility or "regulated" classification. The relative importance of the major groups is indicated by their claimed capital investment and gross revenue for 1931 (with six zeroes omitted):

	CAPITAL INVESTMENT	GROSS REVENUE
Steam Railroads.	24,078	4,500
Electric Light and Power. .	12,400	2,137
Electric Railways.	5,500	1,300
Telephone. . . . . :	4,750	1,200
Manufactured Gas.	3,087	442

94

However, it is electricity which dominates the utility scene. While its claimed invested capital is only half that of steam railroads it is still in its youth. The electrical industry has achieved a solidarity of purpose and action as between its functional units, such as financing, operating, manufacturing, engineering, construction, and contracting; a representation in the major political party organizations; and a control of the means of mass propaganda and ballyhoo which set an all-time record. Its operating companies are as a rule in healthy financial condition and everything suggests that in times anything like normal the saturation-point in the use of electricity would not be in sight. It is in coping with the electrical industry and planning for it that the case of the People *vs.* the Utilities will be won or lost. Obviously, also, if we cannot plan effectively for electricity, it is unlikely that as a people we shall be equal to the task of broader social economic planning.

The enhanced position of electricity in American life is shown by the increase in its use from 110,000,000 kilowatt hours a day in 1921 to 265,000,000 kilowatt hours a day in 1929. This consumption has been divided as between large and small consumers during the five years of 1926-31 as indicated on Chart A. While the small consumers during this period have used but 30 per cent of the current they have contributed 61 per cent of the revenues as indicated by Chart B. On the other hand, the wholesale consumers, that is, the larger industries, the street railways, and the electrified steam railroads, have required 70 per cent of all current sold and yet have yielded only 39 per cent of the industry's total revenues. American industry is 70 per cent elec-

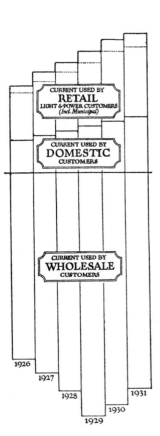

CHART A. WHERE THE
ELECTRICITY GOES

Wholesale customers use 70 per
cent of all the electricity
generated.

(Each inch represents approximately 20 billion K.W.H.)

CHART B. WHERE THE
ELECTRIC REVENUES
COME FROM

Householders and other small
users provide 61 per cent of the
revenues but only use 30 per cent
of the current.

(Each inch represents approximately 800 million dollars.)

trified. That the net revenues of the industry have held up well in the face of a heavy decrease in the use of industrial power tends to prove that the small user is the profitable and reliable consumer.

Practically the whole cost of service to a large consumer lies first in generating the electricity and then in transmitting it on high-voltage lines to the point of use. The cost of this "transmitted current" is of course the same whether delivered to a large industrial establishment or to one of the substations from which the current is distributed over wires of lower voltage to homes and farms. In order to get the entire cost of service to these small-scale users we must add to the cost of the "transmitted current" the capital charges and operating expenses required to put it through the distribution substation and the low-voltage distribution lines to the far side of the customers' meters. This covers the whole cost of domestic service.

There are three classes of electric service into which distribution enters as an important cost factor, that is, domestic; commercial light and power, retail; and municipal, largely street lighting. The current consumed by each class and the revenue derived therefrom in 1931 were as follows:

	K.W.H.	REVENUE
Domestic	11,785,000,000	$686,000,000
Commercial light and power...	13,837,000,000	569,000,000
Municipal and street lighting	2,793,000,000	108,000,000
	28,415,000,000	$1,363,000,000

97

We may assume that the "transmitted current" used in these services cost on the average 1½ cents per K.W.H., including return on invested capital. The national average rate for wholesale transmitted power is 1.42 cents per K.W.H. Municipalities—even small ones —buy power at figures generally ranging from a little over one cent to a little less than two cents per K.W.H. The part of the sales price therefore attributable to 28,415,000,000 K.W.H. of current would total $426,-225,000. Subtracting this from the $1,363,000,000 charged for these services, there remains $936,775,000 to be justified as the cost, including profit, of distribution, or nearly one-half of the total revenues of the industry. If, as suggested by my own studies carried on continuously for nearly twenty years and outlined in "On the Cost of Distribution of Electricity" and elsewhere, this public outlay for distribution is about twice what it should be, we are confronted with an annual overcharge against the small consumer of between $400,000,000 and $500,000,000 a year.

Certainly $900,000,000 a year is far too large a tax to be levied without reasonable proof as to its approximate justice. And yet there is an almost complete absence of anything approximating cost control or even of cost knowledge concerning electrical distribution, and not one generally recognized cost standard. Practices and results obtained in different areas cannot be compared. The usual process of improving methods by setting one up against another is therefore generally missing. Waste necessarily results.

Engineering literature teems with meticulous data on generating costs. We know within narrow limits the cost of transmitting current. But we have no information about an item which is certainly much more important to the small consumer than the costs of generation and transmission combined. The cost of the distribution of electricity, alleged to account for the high rates at which domestic electricity is sold, has never been discussed by any group of professional engineers, and the subject is taboo before every engineering society in the United States. This lack of definite data in regard to distribution costs accounts for the present meaningless multiplicity of rate schedules. Before many years a single rate schedule will cover vast areas.

Through propaganda fostered by the electrical industry the public has been led to believe that domestic electric rates have been "steadily going down." The nationwide average price fell from 7 cents per K.W.H. in 1926 to 6 cents in 1931. This drop in the national average chiefly affects, however, only that very small percentage of customers whose exceptionally large consumption gives them the benefit of low promotional rates. Such lowering of the national average has very little bearing on the trend of rates paid in the majority —possibly 90 per cent—of American homes.

The revenue derived from the average domestic user increases yearly. It was $29.70 in 1926 and $33.70 in 1931. It is highly probable that the industry has secured a greater profit per domestic customer, and per K.W.H. used in domestic service, with each drop in the national average. For in serving the average domestic customer with the small annual increments in the quantity of current indicated in recent years, practically the only added expense is for the current itself. Computing this at 1½ cents per K.W.H. we find that in each of the last five years the amount required to cover the additional current averages only about half the added revenue received.

Until within the last two or three years, except for the supervision of the Interstate Commerce Commission over the railroads, public authority has hardly been felt in the utility world. Barring a few sporadic instances of gentle discipline, and these confined to a few states, the utilities have been allowed to work out their own salvation, if you can call it that. Electrically speaking, Sidney Z. Mitchell was Alpha and Samuel Insull was Omega. An occasional Hopson was the only fly in the ointment. But the substitution by Governor Roosevelt of Maltbie for Prendergast as chairman of the New York Commission, the recent appointment of Lilienthal in Wisconsin, the activities of Seavey in California and of Morse in New Hampshire, and the refusal of the Massachusetts Commission to allow the Boston Edison split-up are happenings which serve to remind the general public of what was originally expected of regulation.

Things have also been occurring in the public-ownership field. When gas and electricity supplies and telephone services were confined to single localities, thousands of such plants were publicly owned. Coincident with the interconnection of these utilities over wide areas, the private interests initiated a process of eliminating the competition of the public plant. More than forty years ago Edison advised the electrical industry to insure the permanency of its investment "by keeping prices so low that there is no inducement to others to come in and ruin it." Because this advice has not been heeded, strong and apparently effective public-ownership currents have been set up in various parts of the country. There are well-managed publicly owned electric plants of considerable size in Seattle and Tacoma, Washington; Los Angeles and Pasadena, California; Springfield, Illinois; Jamestown, New York; Holyoke, Massachusetts; and Jacksonville, Florida. There are at present more than 2,000 such municipal electric plants—most of them quite small.

But far more significant is the legislation already passed in Nebraska, Wisconsin, Washington, and Oregon, and proposed in New York by Governor Roosevelt, to facilitate the tying together of individual municipal gas and electric plants into power districts technically and otherwise able to compete with privately owned superpower systems. All legal barriers against providing a public plant, once the people have voted for it, should be removed. Nothing has proved so effective in securing reasonable rates from the private companies as the realization that the public has this remedy at hand.

Except as to water supplies, public ownership in this country is of the "yardstick" variety. While in any one industry the percentage of public as compared with private plants is low, such public installations as there are exert an important influence in providing the public with the standards by which performance of the private plants can be measured. One of the difficulties in steam railroad regulation has been the entire absence of the opportunity for public experimentation in this field. It is exceedingly difficult to initiate a desirable practice such as cost-finding in the absence of individual units uncontrolled by hard and fast inter-company practices. I am convinced—having elsewhere given my reasons in detail [1]—that it would be a mistake to plan now for widespread public ownership in this country. Rather we should concentrate on the effective operation of a few favorably located installations, large enough to fire the public imagination and to exclude petty politics. The water-power projects at Boulder Dam, on the St. Lawrence, and at Muscle Shoals should be pushed, and experiments should be made in extended but intrastate power districts; these are already under way in western Washington and are being actively planned in Wisconsin.

On the other hand, in the light of the experience during two generations, it would be a mistake to place too much reliance on either federal or State regulation. The Interstate Commerce Commission has on the whole done a remarkably good job in its piloting of the difficult railroad situation. The early adoption of standardized and revealing accounting, reasonable success in keeping politics at a distance, and the presence on the commission almost from the start of some unusually able men are among the contributing causes. But the end seems not far off. Especially in case the depression continues, it appears to be only a question as to how long most of the steam roads can hold out. Bonded as they are to the hilt and with no market for their stocks, the solution will inevitably be public ownership, not because it is desirable in itself, but because it has become

[1] See *National Municipal Review*, November, 1931.

inevitable.[2] Public ownership the world over has usually come by this route.

State regulation of utilities other than steam railroads began about 1907. Up to the recent drop in the price level State regulation was essentially one long battle over regulation—and a losing one for the public. Untold millions collected from the people through rates were expended by lawyers, accountants, "valuation engineers," and a few economists in building up the fictions which made possible the reproduction-cost-new method of valuation. Through hundreds of commission and court decisions and far-flung propaganda this rule has almost—but not quite—become "the law of the land." Curiously and tragically enough, present price levels are forcing the private utility interests to seek quite unceremoniously the abandonment of reproduction-cost-new as a basis for valuation. Under its inevitable findings at present prices even some of the strongest companies would face disaster. Liberals have constantly pleaded for prudent investment as the rate base. Prudent investment has been consistently advocated by Justice Brandeis in classic dissenting opinions, not because it would yield either a high or a low valuation but because without a stable rate base neither regulation nor the efficient operation of utility properties is possible. Whether in the current turmoil a graceful shift from one technique to the other can be made is another question. The adoption of prudent investment now would be a tremendous aid to regulation and is to be

[2] See "A Plan for Public Ownership and Operation," by Joseph B. Eastman. *Annals of the American Academy of Political and Social Science*, January, 1932.

recommended even if it does give valuations higher than indicated by reproduction-cost-new methods. Certainly the United States Supreme Court will have to backwater considerably from its position in the Indianapolis Water and other recent cases to meet the seeming necessities of the situation. In the Baltimore Street Railway case even depreciation was to be figured on the basis of reproduction-cost at current price levels. But the utilities have Justice Holmes's comforting assurance that "words can usually be found in the English language to bridge such difficulties."

The desire of the private interests to avoid valuations made at current prices and of the commissions to avoid the delays incident to expensive and long-drawn-out rate litigation has brought rate-making by conference and mutual agreement to the fore. As a temporary expedient appropriate to the times it has some merit. But as applied to current domestic electric rates the process is not apt to be virile enough in the long run to satisfy the needs of the situation.

But "yardstick" public ownership and regulation will have to be supplemented by fundamental and extensive research conducted under public auspices as a guide to future public planning. There is no such thing as scientific management without unprejudiced research. To meet this need Governor Pinchot suggested a giant power board instructed to study out Pennsylvania's electrical future. This idea has since been carried out in Great Britain by the creation of the Central Electricity Board. It has been effectively active in executing projects looking toward a better planning of Britain's electrical economy—its duties are wholly outside regulation as we know it. The Wisconsin legislature at its last session followed the suggestion of Governor La Follette and provided for a similar board to study the future power needs of the State, to plan the facilities and agencies found to be necessary, and to plot the method for coördinating all public and private power and light activities.

A federal utilities planning board, unhampered by the routine regulatory responsibilities which harass the Interstate Commerce Commission and the Federal Power Commission, and supplemented by similar agencies in a half-dozen States, might in time clarify the questions which keep regulation relatively ineffective. Ability to require the facts in any given situation would be all the power needed by such an agency. The field and function of transmission lines, especially those of the higher voltages, is of the most immediate importance to electrical development. It is highly probable that the cheapest power sources cannot be tapped except by government-owned lines or at least by lines owned by private concerns operating only in the transmission field. This may mean that transmission lines under certain conditions should be given the status of common carriers.

Until recently the ascertainment of the cost of electrical distribution in any given situation seemed all but a hopeless task. With a minimum of detached inquiry it now seems probable that a generally applicable formula can be derived.

An opportunity to reduce electric—and other utility—costs presents itself in the more effective use of our highways by the joint use of poles and the common use of duct or conduit systems or by the construction and common use of underground tunnels or galleries in which are placed conductors and pipes. The joint use of poles—both urban and rural—if fully carried out would alone reduce the present utility investment by nearly half a billion dollars and save fifty millions in annual costs.

The motor-transport industries—street and interurban electric lines, subway and elevated railroads, bus and truck and taxicab operators—struggle more or less blindly to protect and advance special interests when many of the misconceptions upon which their controversies feed could be dispelled by the dispassionate assembly of facts, many of them quite near the surface. Another profitable field for planning inquiry is suggested by the recent rapid development of interstate natural gas lines, now lying, with interstate electrical transmission lines, entirely beyond regulatory control. Several of our public-service commissions have recently instituted research bureaus, but naturally they are chiefly occupied with studies immediately bearing on cases pressing for decision.

Perhaps from the standpoint of national well-being nothing in the utility field is more insistently important than the effective maintenance of a first-class national transportation system binding the several sections of our domain into one operating unit and powered to match our industrial and agricultural development. But this provided for, plentiful, widely distributed, low-cost electricity will in the long run prove to be one of the master indices of our economic, social, and cultural development. We begin to see the manifold ways in which abundant low-cost electricity may directly affect home life. But it is not so clear to industrialists, or to those in the electrical industry itself, how rapidly electricity is permeating our machine age, so that it is becoming an electrical rather than a mechanical age. The first automatic industry is here. The necessity for human effort has entirely disappeared from the generation of electricity. By merely touching buttons we have illimitable power at our disposal. Eight men on a shift watch 500,000 electrical horse-power developed above the Saguenay!

This factor of automaticity is increasing in every industry. The assembly line at the Ford plant with its hustlers at every point is cited as the fine flower of mass production. Yet Henry Ford is quoted as saying that he will promptly transform it into a vast machine requiring no human effort—merely control—as soon as the increased demand for his cars warrants it. Power can spell freedom for the race. But without foresight and planning it may easily be our undoing.

WINTHROP M. DANIELS

is professor of transportation at Yale University. He was a member of the Interstate Commerce Commission from 1914 to 1923.

The Future of the Railroads

THE POST-PANIC period since the fall of 1929 has sufficed to explode a number of illusions as to the future of our railroads. These illusions were entertained from 1920 to 1929, a period in our economic history which is likely to be known as the "fools'-paradise decade." The first legal breakdown came in the midst of this period. This was the elaborate provision in the Esch-Cummins Act of 1920 for the settlement of railroad labor disputes by the tri-partisan Railroad Labor Board. That ill-starred tribunal created a record remarkable for nothing so much as the mutual billingsgate of majority and minority opinion. The opposing factions indulged in an undiplomatic interchange of impolite symbols of mutual distrust, and the board was fortunately snuffed out of existence by a repealer in 1926. The cumbrous legal artillery which was substituted by the Railway Labor Act serves today chiefly as "the gun behind the door," to escape which both parties, when the wage question is grave and urgent, resort to direct conference, as in January of this year. In a sense wholly alien to that in which Lord Mansfield coined the phrase, both management and employees realize that "freight is the mother of wages," and that direct negotiation and adjustments are infinitely preferable to the well-meant but dilatory official routine of settlement.

108

But the futility of this section of the Transportation Act of 1920 has been matched by its demonstrated breakdown in matters of equal importance. Had the Labor Board provision never been made a rider on the other provisions of the law, the country might have anticipated with some considerable confidence that railroad labor disputes and wage controversies would have been adjusted eventually through the voluntary process of collective bargaining. Where the Esch-Cummins Act lulled the country into an unfounded sense of security was mainly in the matter of future railway rates, the anticipated fair return on railroad property, the recapture of excess railway earnings, and the speedy realization of railroad consolidation. Indeed, the only marked exception to the disappointing category of achievements under the new law has been the regulation of railroad security issues—a device long before in use by many State commissions in respect of local public utilities.

There were, of course, no factual data upon which to base the optimistic opinion, expressed in Congressional debate on the act of 1920, that consolidation would bring economies of hundreds of millions of dollars which would be translated into abatements of railway rates and charges. These roseate dreams never had any solid foundation, and the railroads, to do them justice, never made any such pretensions. The fatuous idea seems to have arisen from the conception that railroad operation was like that of a Ford automobile factory, and that if only the plant could be made large enough, the unit cost of product could be correspondingly lessened.

If the shipping public was misled in anticipating

109

marked abatement of rates, the railroad investors were equally disappointed in expecting assured returns on their securities. The so-called "rate-making provision" proved a delusion. "In the exercise of its power to prescribe just and reasonable rates" the commmission was to establish general rate levels such that carriers as a whole were to earn an annual operating income "equal, as nearly as may be, to a fair return" upon the aggregate value of their operating properties. This provision was hailed as the railroads' new Magna Charta. It was supposed to double-track the old single-line Interstate Commerce Act. Before then the act had for its main aim the relief of shippers distressed by unreasonable or unduly prejudicial rates. Thereafter the act was to aim equally at providing annually a fair rate of return upon carrier property as a whole. The law, said the Supreme Court in the Dayton-Goose Creek case, "puts the railroad systems more completely than ever under the fostering guardianship and control of the commission." Investors since the passage of the act have put hundreds of millions of dollars of additional capital in American railroads. Commissioner Woodlock said in a dissenting opinion in 1927: "If any conclusion may fairly be drawn from the fact that capital has been supplied to the railroad industry by investors in the years following 1920, it is the conclusion that in supplying it investors have relied upon the terms of the law, the statements of this commission, and the decisions of the Supreme Court. . . ."

It will be well to consider the causes which precluded the expected realization of the rate provision for a fair annual return on railroad property. Primarily, that provision completely overlooked the cyclical rise and fall in industrial conditions. The demand for the service of transportation is at all times a derivative of the contemporaneous output of general industry. Only to the extent that things are being produced and consumed, are being bought and sold, is there an effective demand for their transport. This has always been true for any considerable period of time, even when no abysmal depression such as the present one has been encountered. The railroad freight tonnage which originated in 1921, for example, fell just 25 per cent below the tonnage of the previous year. The average rate per ton mile, however, was more than 20 per cent higher in 1921 than in 1920; but with major fluctuations of traffic volume the average rate of charge per unit of traffic becomes a factor of wholly secondary importance. Until or unless a substantially constant volume of traffic can be anticipated, no approximate assurance of a virtually constant annual return, gross or net, can be given. In the face of facts only too patent, the Transportation Act of 1920 held forth the expectation that a stable return would be forthcoming. It is hardly necessary to add that what was impossible in a decade of normal ups and downs, became almost tragically ludicrous in an industrial debacle such as the present, when weekly car-loadings are hardly more than 50 per cent of what they were in 1929, and when over three-quarters of the Class I railroads, with normal annual revenues over $1,000,000 each, failed in the first two months of the present year to earn their fixed charges of interest, rentals, and taxes.

The failure for twelve successive years to realize, even in a single year, the fair rate of return points to other factors besides the law's mistaken assumption already discussed. If for a few years out of the last twelve the declared fair rate of return had been exceeded, there would arise a possible presumption that, while no constancy in annual return might be attainable, at least the return might be realized on the average, taking one year with another. Marksmen who for twelve consecutive years invariably shoot below the bull's eye must be chargeable with too low an aim, or with trying to hit an impossible target. The responsibility for the result of continuous failure cannot be put on any one pair of shoulders. The law, the commission, the carriers themselves, Congress, the early distress of agriculture, the expansion of pipe-lines, the enlargement of water carriage, and the growth of motor transport all contributed in various degrees to the result.

The commission began bravely in 1920 to attempt to solve the insoluble problem that the law had set. The first full year under the new and higher rate levels coincided with a marked industrial recession. The return realized was less than half of what the carriers had been led to expect. In 1922 the commission reduced freight rates by 10 per cent in the hope that the reduction would enlarge the tonnage. The railroads made a pro forma protest, but privately admitted that the rate level had been higher than the traffic would bear. While there was no repetition of the cutthroat competition of the early rate-war days, the carriers themselves, in seeking individually to gain traffic or to divert it from other lines, were continually reducing rates. The average revenue per ton mile sank steadily with each successive year. Some of the reductions made by the commission provoked loud outcry from the carriers, but they were doing the same thing themselves. In other cases, where the carriers knew that certain rates were non-compensatory, they were inexcusably dilatory in proposing an advance. The commission's new power of prescribing minimum rates was used most sparingly. Nor was it easy for that body to divest itself of its earlier habit of regarding rates mainly from the shipper's standpoint. In the meantime the pronounced agricultural depression had found a voice in the Hoch-Smith resolution. The commission in conformity therewith discovered that rates recently fixed by it were not at the exact bottom of "the zone of reasonableness," and proceeded to depress them further, and even to grant reparation to shippers who had paid the rates set by the commission itself until the Supreme Court called a halt on this policy of spoliation. Meanwhile the attitude of the commission toward minimizing the valuation on which a return was to be computed was evidenced in the famous O'Fallon case. Apparently the commission has concluded that the rule of rate-making is in abeyance, or in strict subordination to the independent fixing of just and reasonable rates. The assumption of the statute that just rates and fair return are compatible, or the interpretation of the statute to the effect that the resultant return is a regular criterion of justness and reasonableness, has gone by the board. The "fostering guardianship" of the railroads by the commission has evidently not materialized.

It is not necessary to determine in just what degree other factors, such as competition by motor vehicles, by water, or by pipe-line, have coöperated to create the impasse at which the railroads and the commission have arrived. Economic forces more powerful than either have stamped with futility the statute which ostensibly governs them both. The proposed repeal of Section 15a, which contains the rate-making provision, is only a belated recognition of earlier legislative ineptitude. The proposed substitute is a meaningless formula exemplifying the adage that "mistiness is the mother of wisdom." The earlier vituperation against the section as a virtual guaranty of profits, and the earlier homage to the section as "the perfection of reason" and the sheet anchor of the investor, look equally absurd in the grim light of subsequent happenings.

If a legal regulation of return on carrier property is to be again essayed, it might be sought along the line of establishing in advance a basic or standard net operating income for the roads as a whole in each distinct railroad region. There is no reason to suppose that this income would be exactly realized in any particular calendar year. But the defect or excess in such standard earnings might serve as a barometer, exempting the carriers of the region from mandatory or voluntary rate reductions in the period following a deficiency, and entitling the patrons of the roads to rate abatements in the period following excess carrier income. This is the provision in the law in Great Britain, where the 1913 earnings are taken as the standard bench mark, and where the Rates Tribunal makes an annual review of earnings with a view to a recension of the body of rates, as yet, admittedly, without attaining the desired result.

The greater feasibility of such a plan in Great Britain is due to that country's having amalgamated its railways into four systems. It would be facilitated here had our roads been consolidated into a limited number of systems. Of all the prospects held out by the Transportation Act of 1920 none has miscarried so eccentrically as the consolidation project. It is true that large and numerous unifications of control through stock ownership and lease have been effected, with immunity from the anti-trust acts. It is true also that the holding-company device, in extra-legal fashion, may have accomplished the same result, except for the feature of legal immunity. But in no case of major importance has complete consolidation in the strict sense been attained, with its extinction of multitudinous subsidiary corporations, and with full realization of even the limited economies that full-fledged consolidation would permit. For those who are attracted by the modern economic device known as "economic planning," it must be a sobering reflection that a presumably expert commission took almost ten years before promulgating what the statute required—a final plan for the consolidation of the railroads into a limited number of systems. During this period the virus which the consolidation provisions of the law had injected into the veins of railroad men worked ill. Ambitious executives were bitten with the illusion of grandeur, and dreamed of transportation empires worthy of Harriman. Others, fearful of possible dismemberment of their present mileage, or of a blocking of their own cherished plans of annexation or extension, sought through affiliated holding companies to acquire rail securities as trading assets which would strengthen their strategic position. The placement of new shops to be centrally located on the new systems was deferred in some cases, because no one could tell in advance just what lines each system would comprise. Employees saw their rights of seniority and pensions jeopardized by a possible severance from their long-time corporate employers. Short lines saw an opportunity of realizing on their nuisance values by threatening to oppose any plan of unification which did not absorb their properties at inflated purchase prices. Regional racketeering received an impetus by the possibility of intervening in opposition to proposed unifications of lines if the project did not pay tribute to grandiose local aspirations. The commission's "final plan," moreover, embodied some fantastic mergers of lines which stretched from the Missouri River to the Florida Everglades, the chief components of which are at present in the bankruptcy courts. Presidential and Congressional interference in the settlement only intensified the chaos, and the labor organizations, recognizing that many of the economies were to be effected by labor displacements, formed a bloc to checkmate the whole design. No such comedy of errors ever attended what was proposed as a serious economic design.

To effect consolidation with reasonable promptness, the spur of compulsion must be applied. With federal power which is exclusive and plenary over interstate commerce, this should not be an impossible task. The present law conditions the capitalization of the new consolidated systems upon the commission's valuations of their constituent properties. If these valuations are disputed, and they frequently are, the law necessitates an interminable delay. This provision might be advantageously junked, leaving with the commission a sound dis-

cretion to require a capital set-up in each case compatible
with the public interest. The official "plan" of consolidation might also go to the scrap-heap without loss. If
the companies were allowed, or required, to propose
their own plans for consolidation—and the commission
might, as now, exercise a veto over them—we should be
farther along than we are today. We may also wisely
take another leaf from the English statute book by requiring that each consolidation shall provide financially,
as, for example, by pensions, for the displacement of
labor which it occasions. Last of the embarrassing hang-
overs from the present law is the provision for recapture of excess earnings. Here again attempted enforcement invokes a lawsuit, for evidently the existence of
excess earnings can be shown only after the establishment of a legal base on which to make the computation
as to the alleged excess. The failure of the companies
generally to obtain the fair rate of return, and the
prima facie unfairness of recapturing excess earnings in
fat years with no offsets for deficient earnings in lean
years, would seem to make retroactive repeal of the
provision the quickest way out of what was at best a
position of dubious merit.

While the current depression has radically decreased
the demand for rail transportation, the railways have
also been suffering from the rapid extension of the supply of transport services, mainly offered by motor
vehicles. It is only too apparent that in the domain of
passenger conveyance the railroads must be content with
playing a subordinate rôle. With over 23,000,000 reg-
istered private motor cars, the possibility of the railroads
ever regaining their former dominance in passenger

transportation is gone. Long-distance travel and the mass transportation of commutation traffic will doubtless perpetuate some degree of railroad passenger service; but the decline of passenger revenue, both absolute and relative, no less than the increasing railroad operation, either direct or through subsidiaries, of motor buses on the highways, indicates the complete transformation of what was once a rail monopoly.

Truck competition is an even more vital thrust at the railroads, in large measure because rail movements are in a regulatory harness as to the requirement of publishing and observing scheduled rates and conforming to the acts controlling the hours of service of their employees. Even if public interstate buses and both common carrier and contract trucks be eventually subjected to the same regulation as railroads, the private car and the private truck will permanently retain a substantial volume of traffic. The rail companies are keenly alive to the menace of the trucker, and the annexation of motor equipment to their own operative apparatus is a sign that they recognize the inevitable. The growth of motor pick-up and delivery service by railroads, the development of containers readily transferred from the motor chassis to the floor of the flat car, the issuance of container and truck-body tariffs conforming more closely to distance of haul than to the value of freight, the offer of all commodity rates in mixed carloads, all betoken the railroads' response to the challenge of the trucking companies. The carriage of heavy carload freight, particularly for long hauls, is the railroads' least vulnerable citadel. It is difficult to see how this can well be wrested from them, but evidently they do

118

not propose to surrender the outworks of merchandise traffic without a struggle.

The future of rates is to be determined by the inevitable future law of costs. "What the traffic will cost" may not improbably displace "what the traffic will bear" as a transportation watchword. It can hardly be anticipated that the regulatory effort, already apparent in Germany, to restrict road haulage artificially in order to protect rail tonnage or earnings can eventually prevail against advancing technique in the world of transport. It has been proposed to meet the difficult problem of unregulated truck competition by giving to the railroads the same unrestricted powers as the truckers in operating trucks on the highways. It may be urged in opposition that this would enable the railway treasuries to cover the loss on highway operation until the independent trucking companies had been killed off. It would seem preferable to permit rail carriers to acquire substantial interests in large trucking companies and in motor-bus lines, with the anticipation that this arrangement will tend to allocate to rail and highway the traffic which each can most appropriately handle.

The question of our ultimate governmental policy toward railroads, whether by a changed system of regulation or by eventual government ownership and operation, is complicated by the present world-wide depression. If economic recovery is delayed for several years, the possibility of rational choice in the matter may simply disappear. The question will then resolve itself not into the query whether we deliberately prefer governmental ownership, but whether we can avoid it. The holding by insurance companies and mutual savings banks of something like $4,000,000,000 of railway bonds in their portfolios may dictate government advances to the railroads for a time, in order to prevent default on bond interest or maturities. But should these advances grow to an amount of great magnitude, it will be difficult to oppose the proposition that there should be federal representation on railroad directorates. This could easily presage government ownership outright. Security-owners of British railroads are said to be doubtful whether to continue their present status or to exchange their holdings for government bonds which might issue to purchase the properties. It is by no means impossible that a similar tendency might develop in this country. Stock equities in many of our strongest companies have shrunk to almost microscopic proportions. Receiverships have been avoided only by the Reconstruction Finance Corporation's coming to the rescue. We are hardly aware of the extent to which the federal government in this administration of "sturdy individualism" has gone in underwriting private industry. The demonstrated failure of the tariff to help the farmer has compelled the Farm Board to buy up and hold off the market stupendous quantities of wheat and cotton in a vain attempt to peg their prices. The Farm Loan machinery has put its credit at the service of hundreds of thousands of distressed agriculturalists. The frozen assets of hundreds of banks have been taken over into Uncle Sam's bosom, and schemes innumerable for giving Treasury aid to the building trades and to all sorts of enterprises, public and private, swarm in the halls of legislation.

The attitude of railroad labor towards national ownership and operation of railroads, and incidentally the effect on the cost of transportation service by rail, may be judged from recent happenings. On top of a reduction of almost 50 per cent in railroad forces since 1920, a 10 per cent cut in wages was accepted by railroad labor at the beginning of this year. It has taken six months for Congress to make a similar cut in federal salaries, and there has been virtually no reduction in pay-roll employees in the federal service. Is it surprising that the railway worker prefers a protected status in federal employ?

It is questionable whether the railroad managements themselves realize the moral liability they incur in invoking federal aid. "The borrower is servant to the lender," as they are likely to discover to their cost. They may shy at receiverships and reorganizations, and find that they have escaped both at the cost of having permanently become the vassals of the government. The writer believes this would be an irreparable misfortune, but cannot affect to be blind to the threatened outcome.

RAY VANCE

is Chairman of the Board of Trustees of the Mutual American Securities Trust. He was president of the Brookmire Economic Service from 1916 to 1926. He is the author of "Business and Investment Forecasting."

The Problem of the Business Cycle[1]

IT is particularly fitting to discuss the business cycle in connection with this depression because failure to provide against the dangers inherent in business cycles has been, in my personal opinion, the prime cause for the extraordinary length and violence of the depression. In the first place, all warnings issued during 1928 and 1929 were met with ridicule as the opinions of men clinging to an "exploded superstition." In the second place, the same men who refused to take precautions which might have prevented much of the damage are equally stubborn in refusing to recognize the signs that the crisis has about run its course and that what the patient needs is a period of natural convalescence rather than surgical operations on all parts which were ever diseased. These two statements are not based on any discounting of the importance of international debts, inflated bank loans, unwise speculation, or any other cause commonly assigned for the occurrence or for the long continuation of this depression. A combination of physical and financial conditions brought on the panic, and the wreckage of that combination must be cleared away before prosperity can return. The point I wish to make is that the creation of that combination was

[1] Published in *The Nation* of June 29, 1932.

122

the result of human activities, and that the creation of the *causes* was, in itself, the *effect* of a state of mind which considered the danger of another depression negligible *under the current business organization*. Furthermore, the failure to clear away the wreckage in a reasonable time is the direct effect of a widespread doubt that prosperity can ever return until the business organization has been fundamentally altered.

All of this is of practical importance because it goes exactly to the crucial point in judgment of any effort to cure this depression or to prevent another. Of course, it is hard to believe today that business will revive unless some one does "something drastic," but is it any harder than it was to see danger in 1928 or 1929? As a matter of fact, there is just as much nonsense being talked today about the impossibility of revival as was ever talked about the impossibility of a panic. The natural forces which will produce that revival are already at work, with the mass of our population coöperating as unconsciously through their daily acts as they coöperated unconsciously in the bringing on of the panic. Legislative or other conscious efforts must be approved when they help along the natural forces, condemned when they seek some miraculous or unsound way out.

Any attempt to give in the limited space of this article a detailed description of the developments which bring about the end of a depression would be ridiculous. However, we may divide them into two general groups which have a definite time sequence. During the first of these periods almost every business or financial indicator declines. All kinds of property, except cash, are pressed for sale at falling prices. Less of all types of goods, except raw food products and basic minerals, are produced than are consumed. Old debts are paid, or canceled through default, more rapidly than new ones are contracted. Working forces are decreased, salary and wage rates are reduced, and incomes from interest, dividends, rent, or professional services all decline. During this period living costs are lowered but purchasing power falls at least as fast, and fear induces a restriction rather than an increase in standards of living even for those whose incomes would permit an expansion or at least a maintenance of standards.

To a certain extent the change into the next phase is caused by sheer exhaustion of goods available for consumption, but a much more powerful factor is found in the fact that holders of cash begin to fear that never again will they be able to acquire so much property in exchange for their cash. As a result, purchases are made in excess of current supply and the business tide rises as inevitably as it declined. Four characteristics of these purchases tend to bring a turning-point in the business tide:

1. They do not arise from the fact that economies in production have reduced prices relatively below current incomes—every economy in production reduces some one's income by exactly the same amount.

2. They are made from accumulated cash which its owners may use at their own judgment.

3. They are not made merely because prices are lower than before but because the owners of cash fear future prices will be higher.

4. The motive for these purchases is the selfish one of getting the most for one's money rather than any altruistic one of "helping the situation."

In brief, the upswing after any period of depression starts with the reëmployment of idle capital, and that reëmployment occurs when the owners of capital believe that profits rather than losses will follow its use in place of its hoarding.

The interests of capital and labor are never identical, but in a situation like the present they happen to be practically concurrent. For most of us the depression will be over when we have steady jobs at living pay, or when the business activities in which we have invested our money begin to show profits. Profits for capital tend to return more slowly than employment for labor, but during the lagging period capitalists are gaining something, and are looking forward to still greater profits. For example, eighteen months after the bottom of the last great depression—1921—factory employment in the United States was more than 5 per cent *above* the peak of employment during the previous prosperity. By contrast, the year 1923, which opened with this new high level of factory employment, ended with eight out of ten outstanding manufacturing corporations showing profits which ranged from a fraction of 1 per cent to a full 55 per cent *below* the previous peak. However, no one of these corporations failed to show reasonable profits in 1923, and no one of them failed to reach a new peak of earnings before the next depression.

So long as a decline is still in progress, it remains hard to see that foundations for improvement are being laid, but some of the things which precede the end of a depression have already been accomplished. Among them are:

1. A liquidation of speculative positions in securities. With brokers' loans below $400,000,000 (a decrease of more than 95 per cent from the peak) we need worry no more about this factor.

2. Current debts have been sharply decreased. Total bank loans were off over 25 per cent by the end of 1931 and reporting member banks indicate a further decline of 33 per cent by May 1, 1932. Debts on open book accounts and installment purchases are reduced even more sharply.

3. The supply of goods available for consumption has been sharply reduced. With wholesale prices for merchandise off 20 per cent, department-store stocks are off 35 per cent, indicating a physical-volume decrease of 19 per cent; and the supply of other unsold finished products has declined by almost exactly the same percentage. These are record-breaking figures, but the amount and condition of goods in the hands of consumers after two and one-half years of low buying are even more significant.

4. Wage rates and the general overhead of business concerns have been curtailed to a point where profits could be made on relatively small volumes of business.

At least three things, however, are not yet accomplished:

1. An adjustment between long-term or "capital" debts and general price levels. In the rush to do this

with intergovernmental debts, we overlook its impossibility for privately owned bonds and mortgages without wholesale bankruptcies. This will be an overhanging cloud until some inflation, or "reflation" has intervened.

2. With the exception of Great Britain no large nation has readjusted its budget to current conditions. To do this does not require an exact balancing of the budget but does require the drastic cutting of expenses built up through long years of free spending, the placing of heavy taxes, and the distribution of taxes over practically all classes and sections of the country. In spite of the tax bill just passed, I do not believe the real readjustment has been accomplished, or that it will be accomplished on the eve of an election, and I do not believe it will be accomplished except by bi-partisan action.

3. Owners of hoarded capital must be convinced that they face an opportunity for profit in its use. This cannot be accomplished until the other readjustments just outlined are clearly promised, and even then it will take more courageous leadership than is now in sight. However, there is little room for doubt that the leadership will be available as it always has been when conditions were right.

Business men and investors have been told that prosperity is just "around the corner" until the phrase has become a national joke. For that reason it seems worth while to consider first some of the factors of delay. Conditions for revival will probably not be right until after the election in November. Theoretically, this might be extended until the new terms of office begin in March or even later than that, when new legislation can be enacted. The effect of an election, however, reaches business confidence long before it affects actual governmental action. We cannot now forecast the election results, but we can assume that the country will vote for what it wants and will have confidence in the resulting government.

Other factors are not so definite. Intergovernmental debts will probably have to wait for a time when a United States Administration with a fresh mandate from the voters can deal with the governments of Europe, which, fortunately, are of relatively recent selection. Some factors of inflation for commodity prices are already at work in Great Britain and some are being tried in the United States. So far those working in this country have had no effect except to slow up the decline in prices. Actual history of past panics shows that commodity prices usually do no better than that until months after the volume of business has increased, so this factor may be considered as already satisfactory. Summing up these indications and allowing for the fact that it usually takes longer for business to rise than to fall, "prosperity" in the sense of normal business is more than a year away. Even the beginning of the climb promises to be four to six months away unless something is done to hasten the natural progress.

A study of past depressions offers only four ways in which prosperity might be hastened:

1. International governmental debts might be canceled or definitely suspended. This would impose a long-term burden on creditors. Personally, I believe

these debts are largely uncollectable, but it is doubtful whether that opinion will become sufficiently general in time to permit action which will affect this depression.

2. International trade barriers might be lowered. This would be of little value unless by coöperation of practically all countries. Probably no action can be obtained for more than a year.

3. Any individual nation may hasten the process by a realistic readjustment of its budget. This is the opportunity which Congress has not adequately seized. As already explained, no elective body has ever had the courage to do a real job on the eve of an election. The individual voters may well do their part by disregarding party lines to bring in a stronger group of men at the next election, but there is small possibility that the present makeshift tax law or a few grudgingly enacted economies will have the desired effect.

4. A genuine inflation of currency, possibly even the suspension of the gold standard, would bring a quick response. Great Britain has already demonstrated this point. Its longer effect has always been seriously bad, and most economists will agree with the writer that impatience with the slow operation of the inflationary forces already at work is likely to produce transient benefit at the expense of trouble over a long period.

On the whole, the only cycle-control measure being seriously neglected in the United States at the present time is the balancing of federal, State, and local budgets. Other artificial aids to recovery at this point would be more likely to hinder than to help the operation of natural forces which are at work to end this depression.

The emphasis I have laid upon natural rather than artificial means of ending a depression must not be construed as a condemnation of efforts to control the swings of the business cycle. The fact that periods of boom and depression are "natural" to business activity is no more reason for accepting them as right or inevitable than the fact that disease is natural to the human body is a reason for giving up preventive hygiene for the healthy or medical treatment for the sick. The fatal error in our treatment of business cycles has been that we have worked at it only after the damage has been done. The time to have prevented the current depression was between January 1, 1927, and January 1, 1929. During those two years business, banking, and political leadership had their final opportunity to provide against the natural reaction from a long period of business and speculative boom. A whole book has been printed ridiculing these leaders for their public statements during those years, but let us rather study their actual operations in fields where control might have been exercised.

The most natural place to expect leadership in cycle control is from the Federal Reserve System. The most noticeable failure of the leaders of that system occurred in 1927. During that year stock prices showed signs of inflation by soaring to new record heights, while business had difficulty in keeping pace, and private banks showed some conservatism by reducing their rediscounts with the Federal Reserve by $45,000,000, or nearly 7 per cent. In this situation the Federal Reserve contributed to further inflation by voluntarily adding $311,000,000—about 45 per cent—to its open-market

130

purchases and by lowering its rediscount rates ½ of 1 per cent as an invitation to an increase of rediscounts. In the following year member banks took the cue so plainly given by the Federal Reserve. They increased their rediscounts by $474,000,000—81 per cent, and increased their loans to brokers by 42 per cent; and by so doing supported an inflation of stock prices which left common stocks yielding an average of 3.60 per cent from their dividends, while the money borrowed to carry them cost 7.4 per cent for time loans and 8.6 per cent for call loans. The Federal Reserve made a feeble attempt to check the tide by withdrawing $233,-000,000 from the open market and by raising the rediscount rate of the New York Bank to 5 per cent, but this had no real effect on the movement which the Federal Reserve authorities had done so much to start. The movements continued till the very breaking-point of the 1929 panic, but it is really the operations of 1927 and 1928 which represent the type of mistake which must be avoided if the business cycle is to be controlled.

The most important factor upon which "new era" disciples relied for cycle control was construction work, but the record here is little better than in banking. It seems reasonably clear that if construction work controlled by governments and large corporations is to be done in times of depression, it must be postponed in a period of boom activity in other lines. However, no such postponement was even considered. By 1925 construction work of the "controllable" type had reached a new high record, and 1926 showed a 26 per cent increase over that. Surely then, if ever, the time for "saving up" of desirable activity along this line had arrived.

131

Instead, 1927 saw another 4 per cent added to the dizzy record of 1926, and 1928 piled still another 5 per cent increase on top of that. Public utilities and railroads responded gallantly in 1930 when President Hoover called on them to continue unnecessary construction work, but the really needed work of that year had been anticipated during the boom, and the unnecessary work brought disaster to the coöperating corporations and to government finance, with a balance of damage rather than of benefit to the country as a whole.

After covering these mistakes of banking and construction policy, it is pleasant to note one instance in which genuine provision for cycle control was made. When business reached normal in late 1922, the debt of the United States government stood at approximately $23,000,000,000. Tax rates were high and the demand for reduction pressing. Two definite tax reductions were actually made, but the brightest spot in our provision for cycle control has to do with the handling of our federal debt. Every six months saw a net reduction in this debt, and so well was the situation handled that reduction continued until long after the panic had fallen upon business and finance. By December 31, 1930, the total was down to $16,000,000,000—a decline of $7,-000,000,000, or over 30 per cent in eight years. Up to June 1, 1932, the figure was still $4,000,000,000 under the 1922 total and $7,000,000,000 under the extreme peak debt of 1919. If the same wise policy prevails during our next prosperity, the recent increase in federal debt need not be of great moment.

Unfortunately, the record on State debts is not of that character, and the handling of municipal debts was

132

one of the worst features of our failure to prepare for depression. Throughout the entire period of prosperity municipal debts showed a consistent yearly increase, with the result that at the first sharp fall in tax yields a disconcerting percentage of our cities either defaulted or had difficulty in meeting their current bills. A curtailment of expenses in this field is even more pressingly necessary than in the federal budget, and a reduction of debt in the next period of prosperity is even more essential if we are to avoid another such depression as this one.

The conclusions which appear to arise from a study of the current business cycle are:

1. This period of depression is drawing to a close from natural causes and will probably show improvement before the end of this year (1932) without any legislative aids.

2. Balancing of federal, State, and municipal budgets by real economy and by common-sense tax methods would not only hasten the turn but would accelerate the rise after it has started.

3. Any attempt at violent fundamental business or banking changes is more likely to retard than accelerate improvement.

4. Avoidance of another depression of such severity and length is possible if we are willing to begin our efforts at cycle control while prosperity is still with us, but it will involve sacrificing part of the possible temporary profits of that period. If we again insist on dancing the last possible step, we shall again be compelled to pay the fiddler's bill in full.

DATE DUE

GAYLORD			PRINTED IN U.S.A.